HERSHEY'S CHOCOLATE MEMORIES.

Sweets and Treats since 1895

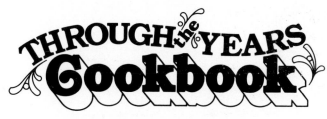

THROUGH the YEARS Cookbook

Nostalgia Author: Nao Hauser
Designer: Tom Gawle
Editor: Cecily R. Hogan

Introduction to *Chocolate Memories* 2-3
1893 to 1909: Candies 4-17
The Teens: Cookies 18-31
The Twenties: Beverages 32-37
The Thirties: Puddings, Ice Creams
    and Other Treats 38-47
The Forties: Pies 48-57
The Fifties: Cakes 58-71
The Sixties: Frostings, Fillings
    and Sauces . . . . ?-79
The Seventies: E . . . . -87
The Eighties: Mi . . . . -95
Recipe Index; S[. . . . .
    Photography (. 96

ISBN 0-943296-00-5

CHOCOLATE MEMORIES®

This book is dedicated to those sweet memories we all have of times and things gone by. Our memories may be of long ago or of yesterday, but with each passing decade certain people, events and styles stand out as those that made the years memorable. To evoke fondest nostalgia "Through the Years" we have sweetened history with a selection of Hershey recipes chosen especially for reminiscing.

Milton Hershey created the legacy of chocolate memories around the turn of the century, when he perfected his formulas for milk chocolate bars, cocoa and baking chocolate. Part of his formula was quality; the other part was low cost to consumers and nationwide marketing. Since his products were available to all Americans, everyone could count a chocolate bar or a chocolate soda, a hot fudge sundae or rich, chewy brownies among their most treasured memories.

These memories have warmed kitchens for generations. At the same time, they have fulfilled each decade's promise of better technology. Chocolate-lovers have never been able to resist the sight of a moist chocolate layer cake gooey with frosting. But chances are the cake proved to be slightly burnt or fallen in the center if it was baked prior to 1915, because up until then the kitchen oven had no thermostat—leaving much to luck and guesswork. And it's safe to speculate that until the 1930's, most cooks who beat the frosting to proper fluffiness had to rest

Above, Milton S. Hershey, 1889; below, a grandma from the "good old days" bakes an oven full of pies!

before they could lift a forkful to their mouth. Even if their homes were wired for electricity—and nine out of 10 farm houses weren't until 1939—they were unlikely to have owned a mixer.

Some memories have faded completely in modern homes, only to be replaced by others. By the end of the 1920's, Grandma could bid good riddance to the ice man who dripped water all over her kitchen floor—that is if she could afford one of the newfangled refrigerators that wore its compressor above the cabinet like a squat, noisy bonnet. At any rate, she had to send Grandpa out to buy ice cream if company was expected, because they couldn't really keep it on hand in the freezer until after World War II.

Today, youngsters might surprise Grandma with their modern expertise about homemade ice cream. For by removing the drudgery of hand cranking, electric ice-cream makers have restored the delights of the creamiest treat. In most households, the whir of a blender can interrupt Grandpa's rambling descriptions of soda fountain treats by producing a much quicker nostalgia trip. And the speed of microwave ovens has put that old tune, "If I Knew You Were Coming," out of style—because you can now bake a cake in the same amount of time it used to take just to make the coffee!

The recipes in this book link the chocolate memories of yesterday with those of tomorrow. You'll find the tastes of microwave chocolate cheesecake and lickety-split cookies as true to tradition as old-fashioned taffy and classic cream pie.

All of the recipes have been developed and carefully tested by the Hershey Foods Test Kitchen. Some are backed with years of tradition; others are all-new Hershey delights. Some are simple kitchen-table treats; others are fancier and include hints for optional garnishes.

We hope you'll enjoy *Hershey's Chocolate Memories* now and in years to come. There are recipes and nostalgic thoughts enough for all to share as you and your family and friends create your *own* chocolate memories.

Today's food enthusiast enjoys a kitchen full of modern convenience!

1893 to 1909

*electricity and turn-of-century technology
pave the way for Hershey Bars . . . and
the best chocolate candies*

When President Grover Cleveland pressed a button to open Chicago's Columbian Exposition of 1893, he revealed a breathtaking spectacle: 633 acres of international exhibition halls lit by thousands of electric bulbs. The excitement drew some 27 million people from all over the world, among them, Milton Hershey, a successful caramel-maker from Lancaster, Pennsylvania.

Hershey shared the amazement of the other visitors who knew only gaslight and candles at home and who were astonished by the rainbow-colored searchlights that swept the fairgrounds at night. They were thrilled by the view from atop the first Ferris Wheel—250 feet up in the air. They stared at Egyptian belly dancers, Venetian gondoliers and African tribal rites. They could hardly believe previews of twentieth century technology—including Thomas Edison's movie projector, the first electric locomotive and a "model kitchen" with a black gas range.

All of this no doubt fascinated Milton Hershey. But what captured most of his attention was a chocolate-making display from Germany. Hershey watched closely as complex machines roasted, hulled and ground cacao beans, then mixed and molded chocolate. He was so impressed that he purchased the invention and had it shipped to his Lancaster Caramel Company when the exposition closed.

Once the equipment was installed in its new home, Hershey hired two expert chocolate-makers to help him create over 100 novelties, including dainty molded chocolates embossed with outlines of chrysanthemums and sweet peas, and fanciful bicycles, lobsters and cigars. All of these items sold well, but only to affluent customers, for they were expensive.

Hershey dreamed of making a chocolate product that everyone could afford. And by the end of 1900 he was ready to act on that dream. In that year, he sold his flourishing company to a rival caramel-maker for $1 million cash. His youth of miserable poverty and repeated business failures was now behind him for good. And the loneliness of those years was gone also, for in 1898 the 41-year-old candy-maker had traveled to New York to marry Catherine Sweeney, a beautiful young woman he had met in the candy shop where she worked.

Free to experiment with the chocolate-making equipment he had retained when he sold the caramel company, Hershey sought a formula that would satisfy his dream. He wanted to turn the bittersweet chocolate of his fancy novelties into a milk-enriched product

*The Ferris Wheel
at the 1893 Chicago
Columbian Exposition*

Milton Hershey's beloved wife, Catherine, in 1898

that could be mass-produced and sold for only a nickel. After hundreds and hundreds of trials, he arrived at the right balance of ingredients as well as suitable techniques. By the end of 1903, he was ready to manufacture Hershey Bars.

His plans to make milk chocolate bars in large enough quantities to hold down the price actually led Hershey to build a town. In Derry Township, around the Pennsylvania farm where he had grown up, he found enough acreage to accommodate both a huge factory and the herds of cows that would be needed to supply it with milk. But he also needed people to make the chocolate. And in 1904, when the factory was completed, he couldn't expect those people to drive cars to work! So it made good sense for Hershey to proceed with what everyone considered his craziest scheme yet: he would turn a thousand acres of cornfields and pasture around the factory into a complete community.

The soda fountain in the Hershey's Cocoa building, 1901 to 1904, in Philadelphia

Since Hershey didn't want a stereotyped "factory town," he insisted that the houses be designed individually and that arrangements be made for workers to own their own homes. Prospective residents were assured of well-paying jobs and modern schools for their children. There was a trolley to transport employees who wished to live, shop or visit in neighboring towns. But the tree-lined streets of Hershey, as the community was named, offered every convenience and amusement—churches, a department store, an inn, a bank, a park, golf courses and even a zoo.

Construction workers didn't have time to complete Milton and Catherine Hershey's own home until the spring of 1908. From the gardens of their mansion—called High Point—the Hersheys could see the lights of the town, where only five years before the meadows had been dark. It must have been a wondrous sight for the dreamer who had marveled at both electric lights and chocolate-making only 15 years before.

5

Gay 90's Pulled Taffy

1¼ cups sugar
¾ cup light corn syrup
⅓ cup Hershey's Cocoa
⅛ teaspoon salt

2 teaspoons vinegar
¼ cup evaporated milk
1 tablespoon butter

Butter a 9-inch square pan. Combine sugar, corn syrup, cocoa, salt and vinegar in heavy 2-quart saucepan. Cook and stir over medium heat until mixture boils; add evaporated milk and butter. Continue to cook, stirring occasionally, to 248°F (firm-ball stage) or until syrup dropped into very cold water forms a firm ball which does not flatten on removal from water. Pour mixture into prepared pan. Cool taffy until comfortable to handle. Butter hands; stretch taffy, folding and pulling until it is light in color and hard to pull. Place taffy on table; pull into ½-inch-wide strips. Cut into 1-inch pieces with buttered scissors; wrap individually. *1¼ pounds taffy.*

Ragtime Rocky Road

2 Hershey's Milk Chocolate
  Bars (½ pound each)
3 cups miniature
  marshmallows

¾ cup coarsely broken
  walnuts or pecans

Melt chocolate bars in top of double boiler over warm water; stir in marshmallows and nuts. Spread in buttered 8-inch square pan. Chill. Cut when firm. *16 squares.*

Gibson Girl Bonbons

1 package (3 ounces)
  cream cheese, softened
2 cups confectioners' sugar
¼ cup Hershey's Cocoa
1 tablespoon plus 1 teaspoon
  melted butter

1 teaspoon vanilla
Columbian Semi-Sweet
  Coating (page 9) or
Easy Semi-Sweet Coating
  (page 10)

Combine cream cheese, confectioners' sugar, cocoa, butter and vanilla in small mixer bowl; blend well. Chill about 1 hour or until mixture is firm enough to handle. Shape into 1-inch balls; place on wax paper-covered tray or cookie sheet. Cover loosely; chill 3 to 4 hours or overnight. Centers should feel dry to touch before coating. Prepare Columbian Semi-Sweet Coating or Easy Semi-Sweet Coating. Remove centers from refrigerator 20 minutes before coating. *About 5 dozen centers.*

Gay 90's Pulled Taffy (wrapped, pulled and ready to cut, cooled and ready to be pulled, cut into 1-inch pieces)

A Most Important Note for Candy Makers

Although Hershey chocolate is tempered during manufacturing, melting destroys this temper. Thus tempering must be repeated by the at-home candy maker. Tempering is achieved by heating and cooling chocolate to specific temperatures so that the chocolate coating will stay firm and glossy.

Carefully read all tips and instructions on pages 8 and 15 before beginning. Set aside about 2 to 3 hours to complete the process. *It cannot be rushed.* Do not try to temper and coat candy on a humid day. Humidity, steam, wet pans or utensils cause chocolate to thicken, tighten and become grainy. Even a few drops of water can cause problems, so make sure that all utensils are dry before beginning.

Candies coated with chocolate that is not tempered will probably have a somewhat sticky coating that will "bloom." Bloom is white or gray spots or streaks caused by separation of the sugar or fat particles from the chocolate. Chocolate that has bloom is not harmful, and it does not taste bad. But it may look unappetizing.

Important Tips!

• The tempering process is not difficult, but it does take time. Remember that "practice makes perfect." It becomes easier each time you do it.

• It is critical that you do not try to rush the process or skip steps. Key words to remember are "slowly," "evenly" and "uniformly."

• The thermometer is critical to the process. Use a thermometer that registers from 70°F to 110°F. Most candy thermometers will not work since they do not register below 100°F; laboratory thermometers do register temperatures in the appropriate range.

• *Important:* The chocolate mixture should be fluid at 108°F. If chocolate becomes tight or grainy due to humidity, stir in a small amount of solid vegetable shortening, one teaspoonful at a time, until chocolate is smooth and fluid again. At this point, retemper chocolate. Do this only as an emergency measure. Do not purposely try to extend chocolate coatings with extra fat and/or water. This will ruin your coating.

• Constant scraping and stirring are necessary for proper crystal formation.

• Use solid vegetable shortening as directed, not butter or margarine. Butter and margarine contain moisture that will cause chocolate to tighten and become grainy.

Columbian Semi-Sweet Coating

2 cups (12-ounce package)
Hershey's Semi-Sweet
Chocolate Chips or
Mini Chips

2 tablespoons plus 2
teaspoons shortening

1. Melt chocolate and shortening in a straight-sided bowl or small mixer bowl set in a pan of very warm water. (Temperature of water should not be above 120°F.)

2. Heat chocolate to 108°F, stirring constantly with rubber spatula; scrape down sides and bottom of bowl frequently so that the chocolate is evenly and uniformly heated.

3. When chocolate reaches 108°F, remove bowl from pan of water. Stir frequently until chocolate cools to 85°F. Continue stirring and scraping bowl constantly until chocolate cools to 80°F.

4. Keep chocolate at 80°F, stirring constantly, for 10 minutes. This is important because it develops the crystals necessary for gloss. It may be necessary to briefly set bowl in warm water to maintain temperature.

5. Rewarm chocolate in pan of warm water to 86°F; hold at that temperature for 5 minutes before dipping.

6. *Important:* Keep chocolate at 86°F during entire dipping process. If temperature at this point goes below 84°F, the entire tempering process must be repeated from Step #2.

7. Centers must be removed from refrigerator and allowed to reach room temperature before coating. (Dipping chilled centers may result in cracked coating and/or bloom on the coating.)

8. Dip room temperature centers or confections completely in tempered, melted chocolate. Dip one at a time with fork, fondue fork, or hat pin. Gently tap fork on side of bowl to remove excess chocolate. Invert onto wax paper-covered tray; immediately swirl small amount of coating over utensil marks.

9. Chill coated candies a maximum of 15 minutes in refrigerator to help coating harden. Remove promptly or bloom may occur.

10. Store coated candies at room temperature (60°-75°F), but keep them well covered.

Milk Chocolate Variation: Substitute 2 cups (11.5-ounce package) Hershey's Milk Chocolate Chips or 8 ounces Hershey's Milk Chocolate Bar and 2 tablespoons shortening. Proceed as directed above.

Vaudeville Nugget Clusters

1 cup Hershey's Milk or Semi-Sweet Chocolate Chips	1 teaspoon shortening 1 cup broken pecans or walnuts

Melt milk or semi-sweet chocolate chips with shortening in top of double boiler over hot water. Remove from heat; stir in pecans or walnuts. Spoon heaping teaspoonfuls into 1-inch paper candy cups or paper-lined mini muffin cups filling each half full. Chill until firm. Peel off paper cup, if desired. *14 to 16 cups.*

Easy Semi-Sweet Coating

1½ cups Hershey's Semi-Sweet Chocolate Mini Chips	2 tablespoons shortening

1. Cover cookie sheet or tray with wax paper; fasten with tape.

2. *Important:* Chop ½ teaspoon Mini Chips into tiny pieces; set aside.

3. Place remaining Mini Chips and shortening in a 2-cup glass measuring cup or 1½-cup wide-mouth jar. Place measuring cup or jar in pan of warm, not hot, water which covers bottom half of measuring cup or jar.

4. Stir constantly until chocolate is completely melted and smooth. (If necessary, keep pan over low heat, but do not allow the water temperature to exceed 125°F.)

5. Remove cup from water; continue stirring until chocolate is cooled to 88°F.

6. Stir finely chopped pieces of Mini Chips into melted chocolate until completely blended. *Note:* This is a vital part of procedure and cannot be omitted. This unmelted chocolate "seeds" the coating and develops the crystals necessary for gloss.

7. Keeping chocolate between 84°F to 86°F dip room temperature centers completely into chocolate, one at a time, with fondue fork, table fork, or hat pin. (To keep chocolate between 84°F and 86°F while dipping, it may be necessary to briefly place jar in warm water.)

8. Gently tap fork or hat pin on side of cup to remove excess chocolate.

9. Invert candy on wax paper-covered cookie sheet; decorate top of coated center with small amount of melted chocolate, using tip of fork or hat pin.

10. Chill coated candies a maximum of 15 minutes in refrigerator to help coating harden. Remove promptly or bloom may occur.

11. Store coated candies at room temperature (60°-75°F), but keep them well covered.

Ferris Wheel Fudge

2 cups (12-ounce package)
Hershey's Semi-Sweet
Chocolate Chips or
Mini Chips
1 Hershey's Milk Chocolate
Bar (½ pound), broken
into pieces
1⅔ cups (13-ounce can)
evaporated milk

1¾ cups (7-ounce jar)
marshmallow creme
4 cups sugar
1 tablespoon butter
1 teaspoon vanilla
1⅔ cups chopped pecans or
walnuts

Combine chips or Mini Chips and chocolate bar in a large bowl; set aside. Combine evaporated milk, marshmallow creme, sugar and butter in a heavy 4-quart saucepan. Cook over medium heat, stirring constantly, until mixture comes to a full rolling boil; boil and stir 8 minutes. Remove from heat; immediately add to chocolate in mixing bowl, beating until completely melted. Blend in vanilla and pecans or walnuts. Pour mixture into a buttered 9-inch square or 13 × 9 × 2-inch pan; cool. *4½ pounds of fudge.*

High Point Fudge Supreme

1 package (8 one-ounce
blocks) Hershey's
Semi-Sweet Baking
Chocolate
1½ cups miniature
marshmallows
½ cup chopped nuts
(optional)

2 tablespoons butter or
margarine
1 teaspoon vanilla
1⅓ cups sugar
⅔ cup evaporated milk
¼ teaspoon salt

Break chocolate blocks into small pieces; place in mixing bowl. Add marshmallows, nuts (if desired), butter or margarine and vanilla; set aside. Combine sugar, evaporated milk and salt in 2-quart saucepan. Stir constantly over medium heat until mixture comes to a full boil. Boil and stir for 3 minutes (if candy thermometer is used, boil until it reaches 225°F). Pour hot syrup over ingredients in mixing bowl; stir until marshmallow and chocolate are completely melted. Pour into buttered 8 or 9-inch square pan. Cool. Cut into squares. *16 squares.*

Double Decker Fudge

1 cup Reese's Peanut Butter Chips	¼ cup butter or margarine
1 cup Hershey's Semi-Sweet Chocolate Chips or Mini Chips	2¼ cups sugar
	1¾ cups (7-ounce jar) marshmallow creme
¾ cup evaporated milk	1 teaspoon vanilla

Measure peanut butter chips into one mixing bowl, and chocolate chips or Mini Chips into second bowl; set aside. Butter an 8-inch square pan. Combine evaporated milk, butter or margarine, sugar and marshmallow creme in a heavy 2¾-quart saucepan. Cook, stirring constantly, over medium heat until mixture begins to boil. Boil and stir 5 minutes. Remove from heat; stir in vanilla. Immediately add about one-half of hot mixture to chocolate chips or Mini Chips, stirring until completely melted; pour into prepared pan. Add remaining hot mixture to peanut butter chips, stirring until completely melted. Spread over top of chocolate layer in pan. Cool. Cut into squares. *About 4 dozen squares.*

Chocolate Kiss Divinity

2½ cups sugar	1 teaspoon vanilla
½ cup light corn syrup	½ cup chopped nuts (optional)
½ cup water	
2 egg whites	30 Hershey's Milk Chocolate Kisses, unwrapped
¼ teaspoon salt	

Combine sugar, corn syrup and water in a 2-quart saucepan. Cook over medium heat, stirring constantly, until sugar dissolves and mixture boils. Cook, without stirring, until syrup reaches 260°F (hardball stage) or until a small amount of syrup dropped into very cold water forms a ball which is hard enough to hold its shape, yet plastic.

Immediately beat egg whites and salt in large mixer bowl at high speed until stiff peaks form. Gradually pour hot syrup in thin stream over egg whites, beating at high speed. Add vanilla and beat until candy holds its shape. Blend in nuts, if desired. Quickly drop candy by teaspoonfuls onto wax paper-covered cookie sheet. Gently press a milk chocolate kiss on top of each piece. Cool; store in airtight container. *About 30 candies.*

Mint Divinity: Omit nuts; add few drops of *either* red or green food color and ½ teaspoon mint flavoring.

(Top to bottom) Double Decker Fudge, Gilded Age Truffles (rolled in confectioners' sugar on left, cocoa on right), Walnut Grove Toffee, Chocolate-Dipped Cherry Cordials, Chocolate Kiss Divinity

Walnut Grove Toffee

1⅓ cups butter or margarine	½ teaspoon baking soda
1 cup sugar	1 cup (5.75-ounce package)
⅔ cup water	Hershey's Milk Chocolate
Dash salt	Chips
⅔ cup chopped walnuts	⅔ cup chopped walnuts

Butter a metal cookie sheet. Combine butter or margarine, sugar, water and salt in a heavy 1½-quart saucepan. Bring to boil over medium heat, stirring constantly. Cook without stirring until mixture reaches 236°F (soft-ball stage) or until small amount of syrup dropped into very cold water forms a soft ball which flattens on removal from water; stir in ⅔ cup walnuts. Continue cooking, stirring constantly, until mixture reaches 290°F (soft-crack stage) or until syrup dropped into very cold water separates into threads which are hard, but not brittle. Remove from heat; stir in baking soda. Turn onto prepared cookie sheet; spread to ¼-inch thickness with a greased knife or spatula. Sprinkle chocolate chips over top of toffee; allow to soften a few minutes. Spread evenly over surface of candy. Quickly sprinkle with ⅔ cup walnuts. Cool several hours or overnight. Break into pieces. *About 30 pieces.*

Chocolate-Dipped Cherry Cordials

¼ cup butter	About 40 maraschino
2¼ cups confectioners' sugar	cherries, drained
1 tablespoon milk	Columbian Semi-Sweet
½ teaspoon vanilla	Coating (page 9) or
⅛ teaspoon almond extract	Easy Semi-Sweet Coating
	(page 10)

Thoroughly cream butter with confectioners' sugar and milk; blend in vanilla and almond extract. (If mixture is too soft, add extra confectioners' sugar.) Mold just enough around each cherry to completely cover cherry. Place on wax paper-covered tray. Cover and chill. Prepare Columbian Semi-Sweet Coating or Easy Semi-Sweet Coating. Remove ⅓ of centers from refrigerator 15 minutes before dipping; keep remaining centers chilled. Dip ⅓ of centers at a time. Store dipped centers, uncovered, at room temperature for four to five days until centers become liquid. *About 5 dozen centers.*

Gilded-Age Truffles

½ cup sweet butter, softened
2½ cups confectioners' sugar
½ cup Hershey's Cocoa

¼ cup heavy cream
1½ teaspoons vanilla
Confectioners' sugar

Cream butter in mixing bowl. Combine confectioners' sugar and cocoa; add alternately with cream and vanilla to butter. Blend well. Chill until firm enough to handle. Shape dough into ¾-inch balls; roll in confectioners' sugar. Store in airtight container in refrigerator. Roll in confectioners' sugar again before serving. *About 36 truffles.*

Party Variation: Decrease vanilla to 1 teaspoon. Add ½ teaspoon rum extract. Roll small amount of mixture around an after-dinner mint, whole candied cherry, whole almond, pecan, or walnut half.

Chocolate Centers

⅓ cup butter or margarine,
    softened
¼ cup heavy cream
1½ teaspoons vanilla
 3 cups confectioners' sugar
½ cup Hershey's Semi-Sweet
    Chocolate Chips or
    Mini Chips, melted

Columbian Semi-Sweet
Coating (page 9) or
Easy Semi-Sweet Coating
(page 10)

Combine butter or margarine, heavy cream, vanilla and 1 cup confectioners' sugar in small mixer bowl; beat until smooth. Gradually blend in remaining confectioners' sugar and chocolate. Chill about 1 hour or until mixture is firm enough to handle. Shape into 1-inch balls; place on wax paper-covered tray or cookie sheet. Cover loosely; chill 3 to 4 hours or overnight. Centers should feel dry to touch before coating. Prepare Columbian Semi-Sweet Coating or Easy Semi-Sweet Coating. Remove centers from refrigerator 20 minutes before coating. *About 5 dozen centers.*

Variations: Divide mixture into three parts. Add ⅓ cup flaked coconut or 1/8 teaspoon peppermint extract or ¼ teaspoon rum extract to thirds of mixture as desired.

Thermometer Tips

Important: Test your thermometer for accuracy by placing it in a pan of boiling water. An accurate thermometer will register 212°F at sea level. If necessary, add or subtract degrees from recipe cooking temperatures according to the thermometer reading in your test.

To get an accurate reading, be sure that your candy thermometer is standing upright and that the bulb is covered by liquid. The bulb should not be resting on the bottom of the pan.

Trolley Car Nougat Chews

1 cup sugar	2 teaspoons vanilla
⅔ cup light corn syrup	2 cups chopped walnuts
2 tablespoons water	4 to 5 drops red food color
¼ cup egg whites (about 2),	(optional)
room temperature	1 cup Hershey's Semi-Sweet
2 cups sugar	Chocolate Mini Chips
1¼ cups light corn syrup	Chocolate Coating
¼ cup butter or margarine,	(recipe below)
melted	Walnut halves (optional)

Line a 15½ × 10½ × 1-inch jelly roll pan with aluminum foil; butter foil. Combine 1 cup sugar, ⅔ cup corn syrup and water in a small heavy saucepan. Place over medium heat, stirring constantly, until sugar dissolves. Cook without stirring. When syrup reaches 230°F, start beating egg whites in large mixer bowl; beat until stiff, but not dry. When syrup reaches 238°F (soft-ball stage) or a small amount of syrup dropped into very cold water forms a soft ball which flattens on removal from water, add syrup in a thin stream to beaten egg whites, beating constantly with mixer at high speed. Continue beating 4 to 5 minutes or until mixture becomes very thick. Cover and set aside.

Combine 2 cups sugar and 1¼ cups corn syrup in a heavy 2-quart saucepan. Place over medium heat, stirring constantly, until sugar dissolves. Cook, without stirring, to 282°F (soft-crack stage) or until a small amount of syrup dropped into very cold water separates into threads which are hard, but not brittle. Pour hot syrup all at once over reserved mixture in bowl; blend with a wooden spoon. Stir in butter or margarine and vanilla; add nuts and blend thoroughly. Add red food color, if desired. Pour into prepared pan. Sprinkle evenly with Mini Chips. Let cool overnight. To form into logs, invert pan and remove foil. Cut in half crosswise; roll from cut end jelly roll style. Spoon Chocolate Coating over roll. Garnish with walnut halves, if desired.

Note: Nougat can be cut into 1-inch squares rather than rolled.

Chocolate Coating

1 cup Hershey's Semi-Sweet	1½ teaspoons shortening
Chocolate Mini Chips	

Melt Mini Chips and shortening in top of double boiler over hot, not boiling, water. Remove pan from hot water and spoon over nougat roll.

the Teens

America grows up with snapshots,
nickelodeons, the Model T . . . and
chocolate cookies warm from the oven

The whole town of Hershey turned out for a grand parade in the spring of 1913. Banners, brass bands and decorated floats celebrated ten years of remarkable success.

Since the blustery day in March when construction had begun, the chocolate factory had been forced to expand to four times its original size. The company had grown from 100 to 1400 employees. And the town could now boast a railroad station, a post office, a theater, a weekly newspaper and a delightful 150-acre park

Watching the parade and waving flags from their open-top gasoline buggy, Milton and Catherine Hershey

looked the picture of proud Americans—he in a straw boater hat and she in an "S-curve" dress with froufrous at the neckline. The Hersheys posed for a photograph with all the pomp and rigidity considered camera-proper then, but the hint of a grin on Catherine's face indicated how happy they must have been.

Photographs captured parades and processions all over America during the teens. Cameras—priced at about $2— were available to most families now. So if the household acquired a brand-new Model T Ford—the price of which fell from $850 in 1908 to $360 in 1916— someone could snap a picture of Papa behind the wheel. If Mama decided that what this country needed was a ban on alcoholic beverages, Papa could photograph her marching down Main Street with the Women's Christian Temperance Union. Maybe Junior took Sis's picture when she went off to join the tens of thousands of other women who rallied for the right to vote in 1914 and 1915. Certainly the family cherished the photo of Junior in his doughboy uniform when he went off to fight the Germans. And when the Great War ended and President Woodrow Wilson announced the armistice on November 11, 1918, everyone saved snapshots of welcome-back hugs and crowds smiling and crying in the streets.

Afterwards, some people said that America "grew up" during the teens. By this, they meant that the nation had engaged in its first major battles outside the western hemisphere and had attained the status of world power. Another milestone they cited was

Above, a Model T Ford;
below, a scene from a
Keystone Kops movie

Armistice Day, November 11, 1918, New York City

Henry Ford's introduction of assembly-line efficiency to the auto industry, as well as his startling announcement in 1914 that he would double his employees' wages to $5 a day. As four million Ford "tin lizzies" hit the nation's unpaved roads—and sank in the mud, as often as not!—another sign of change appeared: women went to work in offices, many of them replacing men as secretaries, typists and telephone operators.

Children reaped unprecedented rewards while America was growing up. The theories of progressive education popularized by John Dewey and Maria Montessori softened the stern rule of school marms. Adolescents won the sympathy of millions of adults who chuckled over the everyday growing pains of the hero of Booth Tarkington's bestselling novel, *Penrod.* Between 1910 and 1920, toy sales tripled, as youngsters added Erector sets, miniature cars and Raggedy Ann dolls to their treasuries of tops, marbles, jacks and hoops.

The whole family found amusement at the picture show, where a nickel or a quarter bought admission to the zany antics of Charlie Chaplin, Fatty Arbuckle, Ben Turpin and Max Sennett's Keystone Kops. In 1916, Mary Pickford commanded a salary of $10,000 a week and acquired the title of "America's Sweetheart."

Rival sweethearts appeared on Broadway in the series of revues called "Ziegfeld Follies," which also showcased the talents of Will Rogers, Eddie Cantor and W.C. Fields. But few entertainers caused quite as much stir as Vernon and Irene Castle, whose graceful ballroom style sent thousands of Americans back to dancing school to learn the latest steps.

Milton Hershey might have settled back to watch young people perform the "turkey trot" and the "bunny hug" at the pavilion in Hershey Park. But he had planned the town and celebrated its success with Catherine at his side, and after she died in 1915, he had to get away for a while. He went to Cuba for a change of scenery, and there he found work that would engage him for several years. By the end of the decade, Hershey, Pennsylvania, had a sister town in Cuba called Central Hershey. Its center was Sugar House, a refinery surrounded by houses, schools and parks for the people who harvested and processed the sugar.

The beautiful tropical gardens of Central Hershey must have reminded the chocolate-maker of his wife, who had planted the rose gardens of Hershey, Pennsylvania. For Milton Hershey remembered Catherine lovingly for 30 years after she died, and he never remarried.

Hershey's Chocolate Chip Cookies

1 cup butter or margarine, softened
¾ cup packed brown sugar
¾ cup sugar
2 eggs
1 teaspoon vanilla
2¼ cups unsifted all-purpose flour

1 teaspoon baking soda
½ teaspoon salt
2 cups (12-ounce package) Hershey's Semi-Sweet Chocolate Chips
1 cup chopped nuts

Cream butter or margarine, brown sugar, sugar, eggs and vanilla in large mixer bowl until light and fluffy. Combine flour, baking soda and salt; add to creamed mixture. Stir in chocolate chips and nuts. Drop by teaspoonfuls onto ungreased cookie sheet. Bake at 375°F for 8 to 10 minutes or until light brown. Cool slightly; remove from cookie sheet onto wire rack. Cool completely.
About 6 dozen cookies.

Tropical Gardens Cookies

½ cup butter or margarine
½ cup shortening
1 cup sugar
¼ cup packed brown sugar
1 teaspoon vanilla
1 egg
1 tablespoon grated orange peel
2¾ cups unsifted all-purpose flour

1½ teaspoons baking soda
1 teaspoon salt
¼ cup orange juice
1¼ cups Hershey's Semi-Sweet Chocolate Mini Chips
Sugar

Cream butter or margarine, shortening, sugar, brown sugar and vanilla until light and fluffy. Add egg and orange peel; blend well. Combine flour, baking soda and salt; add alternately with orange juice to creamed mixture. Stir in Mini Chips. Chill dough about 1 hour. Shape dough into 1-inch balls; roll in sugar. Place on ungreased cookie sheet and flatten with fork. Bake at 350°F for 8 to 10 minutes or until lightly browned. Cool slightly. Remove from cookie sheet; cool on wire rack. *About 7 dozen cookies.*

General Baking Hints

• Ingredients should be at room temperature for the best baking results.

• Never measure ingredients directly over the mixing bowl.

• Measure liquids in a liquid measuring cup and read the amounts at eye level.

Hershey's Chocolate Chip Cookies

Lickety-Split Drop Cookies

1 cup sugar
⅓ cup butter or margarine
1 egg
2 ounces Hershey's
  Unsweetened Baking
  Chocolate, melted
½ teaspoon vanilla

⅔ cup unsifted all-purpose
  flour
¼ teaspoon baking soda
¼ teaspoon salt
1 cup chopped walnuts
  (optional)
Walnut halves (optional)

Combine sugar, butter or margarine and egg in small mixer bowl; beat until well blended. Add chocolate and vanilla; blend well. Combine flour, baking soda and salt; add to chocolate mixture. Stir in chopped nuts, if desired. Drop by teaspoonfuls onto ungreased cookie sheet. Garnish each with walnut half, if desired. Bake at 350°F for 10 minutes or until set. Cool slightly; remove from cookie sheet onto wire rack. Cool completely. *About 3 dozen cookies.*

Tin Lizzie Oatmeal Treats

1 cup shortening
1⅓ cups sugar
2 eggs
2 cups unsifted all-purpose
  flour
⅓ cup Hershey's Cocoa

1 teaspoon baking soda
1 teaspoon salt
1 teaspoon cinnamon
½ cup milk
2 cups rolled oats
1 cup raisins

Cream shortening and sugar in mixer bowl. Add eggs; blend well. Combine flour, cocoa, baking soda, salt and cinnamon; add alternately with milk to creamed mixture. Beat well after each addition. Stir in oats and raisins. Drop by teaspoonfuls onto lightly greased cookie sheet. Bake at 350°F for 10 to 12 minutes. Cool 1 minute. Remove from cookie sheet; cool on wire rack. *About 6 dozen cookies.*

Double Chocolate Hits

⅔ cup butter or margarine
1 cup sugar
1 egg
1 teaspoon vanilla
½ cup Hershey's Cocoa
½ cup buttermilk or water

1¾ cups unsifted all-purpose
  flour
½ teaspoon baking soda
½ teaspoon salt
1 cup Hershey's Semi-Sweet
  Chocolate Mini Chips

Cream butter or margarine, sugar, egg and vanilla in mixer bowl until well blended. Combine cocoa and buttermilk or water in small bowl until smooth; add to creamed mixture. Add flour, baking soda and salt, beating just until blended. Stir in Mini Chips. Drop dough by teaspoonfuls onto ungreased cookie sheet. Bake at 350°F for 8 to 10 minutes or until centers are not quite set. Remove from cookie sheet onto wire rack; cool. *About 4 dozen cookies.*

Chocolate Cream Cheese Brownies

1 cup butter or margarine, softened	1 cup unsifted all-purpose flour
1 package (3 ounces) cream cheese, softened	¾ cup Hershey's Cocoa
	¼ teaspoon baking powder
2 cups sugar	½ teaspoon salt
3 eggs	¾ cup chopped nuts
1 teaspoon vanilla	

Cream butter or margarine, cream cheese and sugar in large mixer bowl. Add eggs and vanilla; blend well. Combine flour, cocoa, baking powder and salt; gradually add to creamed mixture beating until well blended. Stir in nuts. Spread in a greased 13 × 9 × 2-inch pan. Bake at 350°F for 30 to 35 minutes or until brownie begins to pull away from edges of pan. Cool; frost, if desired. Cut into squares. *24 brownies.*

Cocoa Kiss Cookies

1 cup butter or margarine, softened	¼ cup Hershey's Cocoa
	1 cup finely chopped pecans
⅔ cup sugar	9-ounce package Hershey's Milk Chocolate Kisses, about 54
1 teaspoon vanilla	
1⅔ cups unsifted all-purpose flour	Confectioners' sugar

Cream butter or margarine, sugar and vanilla in large mixer bowl. Combine flour and cocoa; blend into creamed mixture. Add nuts; beat on low speed until well blended. Chill dough about 1 hour or until firm enough to handle. Meanwhile, unwrap Kisses. Shape scant tablespoon of dough around a chocolate kiss covering kiss completely. Shape into balls; place on ungreased cookie sheet. Bake at 375°F for 10 to 12 minutes or until set. Cool slightly; remove from cookie sheet onto wire rack. Cool completely; roll in confectioners' sugar. Roll in confectioners' sugar again before serving, if desired. *About 54 cookies.*

Cookie Cues

• Grease a cookie sheet or pan by dipping a piece of wax paper or plastic wrap into shortening and rubbing it evenly over cookie sheet or pan. Do not use butter or margarine.

• Be sure to check cookies at the minimum baking time given. Under-baking results in a soft, doughy cookie; over-baking results in a dry, hard cookie.

• Make cookies in each batch the same size to assure even baking.

• Cookie dough should be placed on a cool cookie sheet; cookies will spread before baking if sheet is hot.

"Uncle Sam-wiches"

½ cup butter or margarine
1 cup sugar
1 egg
1 teaspoon vanilla
1¼ cups unsifted
   all-purpose flour

½ cup Hershey's Cocoa
¾ teaspoon baking soda
¼ teaspoon salt
Creamy Filling
   (recipe below)

Cream butter or margarine, sugar, egg and vanilla until fluffy. Combine flour, cocoa, baking soda and salt; add to creamed mixture. Shape dough into two 1½-inch thick rolls. Wrap in wax paper; chill several hours. Cut into 1/8-inch slices. Place on ungreased cookie sheet. Decorate by drawing tines of fork across each slice. Bake at 375°F for 8 to 10 minutes or until almost firm. Remove from cookie sheet; cool on wire rack. Spread bottom of one cookie with a scant tablespoon of Creamy Filling; top with second cookie.
About 3 dozen sandwich cookies.

Creamy Filling

2½ cups confectioners' sugar
¼ cup butter or margarine,
   softened
2 tablespoons milk

1 teaspoon vanilla
Red or green food color
   (optional)

Combine ingredients except food color in small bowl. Beat until spreading consistency. If desired, divide filling in half; tint ½ pink, tint remaining half pastel green.
Flavor Variations: Add strawberry extract to pink filling and add mint extract to green filling.

How to Melt Chocolate

• Melt milk chocolate in the top of a double boiler over warm water.
• Melt semi-sweet chocolate in the top of a double boiler over hot, not boiling, water.
• Melt unsweetened baking chocolate in the top of a double boiler over simmering water.

(Top to bottom) "Uncle Sam-wiches," Chocolate Thumbprint Cookies (some prepared "festive style" with walnuts, pecans and Hershey's Milk Chocolate Kisses), Silk Stocking Almond Cookies (on left), Chocolate Thumbprint Cookies (on right)

Silk Stocking Almond Cookies

½ cup butter or margarine
½ cup sugar
½ teaspoon vanilla
¼ teaspoon almond extract
1 egg
1½ cups unsifted
   all-purpose flour

½ teaspoon salt
½ cup ground almonds
½ cup chopped candied
   cherries
Chocolate Coating
   (recipe below)

Cream butter or margarine, sugar, vanilla and almond extract in small mixer bowl. Add egg; blend well. Blend in flour and salt; stir in almonds and candied cherries. Divide dough in half and shape into 2 oval-shaped rolls 1½ inches by 2 inches and about 7 inches long; wrap tightly. Chill at least 3 to 4 hours or until firm enough to slice easily. Cut rolls into 1/8-inch slices. Place on ungreased cookie sheet; bake at 375°F for 6 to 8 minutes or until light brown. Immediately remove from cookie sheet; cool. Prepare Chocolate Coating.

Chocolate Coating

1 cup Hershey's Semi-Sweet
   Chocolate Mini Chips

4 ounces Hershey's Milk
   Chocolate Bar
1 tablespoon shortening

Combine Mini Chips, milk chocolate bar and shortening in top of double boiler over hot, not boiling, water. Stir to blend well. Remove top of double boiler from heat; cool to lukewarm. Dip ends of cookies into chocolate; place on wax paper-covered tray. Place in refrigerator about 5 minutes to set chocolate. Remove from refrigerator and holding cookie in center dip other end. Return to tray and refrigerate to set. Store in a cool place.
About 5 dozen cookies.

Cookie Classifications

Drop Cookie: Soft dough is dropped by teaspoonfuls onto cookie sheet.

Bar Cookie: Rich dough is spread in a pan, then baked, cooled and cut into bars or squares.

Molded Cookie: Dough is rolled between palms of hands into desired shapes before baking.

Refrigerator Cookie: Rich, soft dough is shaped into rolls, then chilled thoroughly before cutting into slices for baking.

Rolled Cookie: Soft dough is chilled thoroughly, rolled with a rolling pin on flour-dusted surface, then cut with cookie cutters.

No-Bake Cookie: A molded cookie that has cookie or cracker crumbs or cereal as its basic ingredient and requires no baking.

Press Cookies: Dough is pushed through a cookie press to obtain desired shape before baking.

Chocolate Thumbprint Cookies

½ cup butter or margarine	⅓ cup Hershey's Cocoa
⅔ cup sugar	¼ teaspoon salt
1 egg yolk	Sugar
2 tablespoons milk	Vanilla Filling
1 teaspoon vanilla	(recipe below)
1 cup unsifted	½ cup walnut or pecan halves
all-purpose flour	

Cream butter or margarine, ⅔ cup sugar, egg yolk, milk and vanilla in small mixer bowl. Combine flour, cocoa and salt; blend into creamed mixture. Chill dough at least 1 hour or until firm enough to handle. Roll dough into 1-inch balls. Roll in sugar. Place on lightly greased cookie sheet. Press thumb gently in center of each cookie. Bake at 350°F for 10 to 12 minutes or until set. As soon as cookies are removed from oven, spoon about ¼ teaspoon filling in "thumbprint." Gently place walnut or pecan halves in center. Carefully remove from cookie sheet; cool on wire rack. *26 cookies.*

Vanilla Filling: Thoroughly combine ½ cup confectioners' sugar, 1 tablespoon butter, 2 teaspoons milk and ¼ teaspoon vanilla.

Festive Thumbprint Cookies: Dip 1-inch balls of cookie dough into 1 beaten egg white; then roll balls in a mixture of 1 cup chopped nuts or crushed corn cereal and 2 tablespoons sugar. Bake and fill as above. Instead of garnishing with nuts, gently press an unwrapped Hershey's Milk Chocolate Kiss in center of each cookie.

Bunny Hug Brownies

½ cup sugar	1 teaspoon vanilla
¼ cup evaporated milk	¾ cup unsifted all-purpose
¼ cup butter or margarine	flour
1 package (8 one-ounce	¼ teaspoon baking soda
blocks) Hershey's	¼ teaspoon salt
Semi-Sweet Baking	¾ cup chopped nuts
Chocolate	(optional)
2 eggs	

Combine sugar, evaporated milk and butter or margarine in saucepan. Cook over medium heat, stirring occasionally, until mixture reaches a full boil. Remove from heat; add chocolate (broken into pieces), stirring until melted. Beat in eggs and vanilla. Add flour, baking soda and salt; mix until smooth. Blend in nuts, if desired. Pour into greased 9-inch square pan. Bake at 325°F for 30 to 35 minutes or until brownie begins to pull away from edges of pan. Cool; frost, if desired. Cut into squares. *16 brownies.*

Mini Chip Brownies

½ cup butter or margarine
1 cup packed light brown
    sugar
1 egg
1 teaspoon vanilla

1 cup unsifted all-purpose
    flour
½ teaspoon salt
1 cup Hershey's Semi-Sweet
    Chocolate Mini Chips

Melt butter or margarine in small saucepan; stir in brown sugar. Remove from heat; pour into small mixer bowl. Cool. Beat egg and vanilla into cooled mixture. Add flour and salt, mixing just until well blended. Stir in Mini Chips. Spoon into greased 8 or 9-inch square pan. Bake at 350°F for 25 to 30 minutes or until brownie begins to pull away from edges of pan. Cool; frost, if desired. Cut into squares. *16 brownies.*

Chewy Homestead Brownies

½ cup butter or margarine
1 cup sugar
2 eggs
1 teaspoon vanilla
1¼ cups unsifted
    all-purpose flour

¼ cup Hershey's Cocoa
¼ teaspoon baking soda
¾ cup Hershey's Chocolate
    Flavored Syrup
1 cup Reese's Peanut Butter
    Chips (optional)

Cream butter or margarine, sugar, eggs and vanilla in large mixer bowl. Combine flour, cocoa and baking soda; add alternately with chocolate syrup to creamed mixture. Stir in peanut butter chips, if desired. Spread in greased 13 × 9 × 2-inch pan or 9-inch square pan for thicker brownies; bake at 350°F for 40 to 45 minutes or until brownie begins to pull away from edges of pan. Cool in pan; frost, if desired. Cut into squares. *24 brownies.*

How to Measure Ingredients

Measure Hershey's Cocoa by spooning it into a measuring cup, then leveling it with a spatula or knife. Measure unsifted all-purpose flour the same way. Measure brown sugar by packing it firmly into a dry measuring cup with the back of a spoon. When the sugar is turned out of the cup, the sugar should hold its shape.

Measure shortening by packing it firmly into a dry measuring cup with a spatula. This technique eliminates air pockets. Measure butter or margarine by using the indicators on the wrapper.

*(Left to right) Mini Chip Brownies,
Chewy Homestead Brownies
(frosted), Nickelodeon Peanut
Butter Bars*

Nickelodeon Peanut Butter Bars

⅔ cup butter or margarine
⅔ cup shortening
1 cup sugar
1 cup packed light brown
   sugar
2 teaspoons vanilla
4 eggs
2½ cups unsifted all-purpose
   flour

½ cup Hershey's Cocoa
1 teaspoon baking powder
1 teaspoon salt
2 cups (12-ounce package)
   Reese's Peanut Butter
   Chips

Cream butter or margarine, shortening, sugar, brown sugar and vanilla in large mixer bowl. Add eggs, one at a time, beating well after each addition. Combine flour, cocoa, baking powder and salt; gradually blend into creamed mixture. Stir in peanut butter chips. Spread mixture in two greased and floured 9-inch square pans. Bake at 350°F for 30 to 35 minutes or until cake tester inserted comes out clean. Cool in pan; cut into bars. *About 32 bars.*

Sugar House Frosted Cookies

½ cup butter or margarine,
   softened
1 cup sugar
1 egg
¼ cup milk
1 teaspoon vanilla
1½ cups unsifted all-purpose
   flour

½ cup Hershey's Cocoa
½ teaspoon baking soda
½ teaspoon salt
Sugar
Walnut halves

Combine butter or margarine, 1 cup sugar and egg in large mixer bowl; beat in milk and vanilla. Add flour, cocoa, baking soda and salt; blend well. Chill dough 30 minutes or until easy to handle. Shape dough into 1-inch balls; roll in sugar; top with walnut half. Place on ungreased cookie sheet; bake at 375°F for 8 to 10 minutes or until almost no imprint remains when touched lightly. Immediately remove from cookie sheet; cool on wire rack.
About 3 dozen cookies.

Brown-Eyed Susans

¾ cup butter or margarine
½ cup sugar
1 egg
1 teaspoon vanilla
1⅔ cups unsifted all-purpose
flour
¼ teaspoon salt
Chocolate Filling
(recipe below)
Almonds

Cream butter or margarine, sugar, egg and vanilla in small mixer bowl until fluffy. Add flour and salt; blend well. Shape dough into 1-inch balls (chill if too soft to handle). Place on ungreased cookie sheet. Make indentation in center with thumb. Bake at 375°F for 8 to 10 minutes or until firm and lightly browned. Fill with teaspoonful of Chocolate Filling. Swirl with spatula; top with an almond. Remove from cookie sheet; cool on wire rack. *About 2½ dozen cookies.*

Chocolate Filling: Combine 1 cup confectioners' sugar, 3 tablespoons Hershey's Cocoa, 2 tablespoons butter or margarine, 1½ tablespoons milk and ½ teaspoon vanilla; blend until smooth and creamy.

Celebration Fudgey Brownies

½ cup butter or margarine
2½ ounces Hershey's
Unsweetened Baking
Chocolate
2 eggs
1 cup sugar
½ teaspoon vanilla
½ cup unsifted all-purpose
flour
¼ teaspoon baking powder
¼ teaspoon salt
½ cup chopped nuts

Melt butter or margarine in small saucepan over low heat; add chocolate and stir constantly until melted. Set aside to cool.

Beat eggs in small mixer bowl; add sugar, vanilla and cooled chocolate mixture, beating well. Combine flour, baking powder and salt; blend into chocolate mixture. Add chopped nuts; pour into greased 8-inch square pan. Bake at 350°F for 30 to 35 minutes or until brownie begins to pull away from edges of pan. Cool; frost, if desired. Cut into squares. *16 brownies.*

A Hershey Frosting Hint

One cup frosts one:

8-inch round or square cake
9-inch round or square cake
13 × 9 × 2-inch oblong cake

Two cups frost and fill one:

8 or 9-inch layer cake
A batch of 30 cupcakes

31

the Twenties

the Jazz Age sets the pace for flappers,
flagpole sitters, trans-Atlantic flight . . .
and frothy chocolate beverages

America entered the twenties in the throes of the post-World War I recession and ended the decade on the brink of the Great Depression. But in between, some people had a very good time!

It was a boom time for bootleggers, whose business took off after January of 1920 when the Eighteenth Amendment made prohibition the law of the land. And it was a time of recognition for many great American jazz artists, including King Oliver, Louis Armstrong, Duke Ellington, Bessie Smith and Ethel Waters, who brought the sounds of New Orleans north to the nightclubs and speakeasies of Chicago and New York. Indeed, the musicians often were hired not only to entertain tippling patrons, but also to drown out the backroom violence of rival bootlegging gangsters.

Although women gained the right to vote in 1920 with the passage of the Nineteenth Amendment, in the twenties they became better known for daring fashions than for decisive politics. The Jazz Age flapper had her hair bobbed to ear length and her dresses hemmed to the knee. Corsets were out—so diets were in. A coy "sheba" displayed her "gams" in rolled stockings, pulled a "spiffy" cloche over her shorn locks and hoped that the young "sheik" she was "stuck on" would take her to a "swanky" place, where they could swill "hooch," dance the shimmy or the Charleston—and converse in the "peppy" slang that was all the rage.

Even if the young couple were staid teetotalers, there were more than enough fads and fancies for them to share. Chances were he owned a "jalopy," for one out of every five Americans did by the end of the decade. They could ogle Rudolph Valen-tino and Pola Negri in the old silent movies, or marvel at the "talkies" that arrived in 1927 with *The Jazz Singer.* They could stay home and listen to the radio, which was found in three million households in 1922 and 12 million by 1930. Or they could play two newly available games, contract bridge and Chinese mah-jongg.

If the young couple discussed marriage, the woman could look forward to a life made somewhat easier than her mother's by the advent of vacuum

Above, a "flapper;"
below, a 1928 parade in
Brooklyn, NY, for pilot
Charles A. Lindbergh

King Oliver's jazz band, including Louis Armstrong and Joe ("King") Oliver (4th and 5th from left)

cleaners, washing machines and, by the end of the decade, electric refrigerators. The young man could dream of making a fortune, for reports were rife in the twenties of stock market profits gone wild. And if he didn't strike it rich, they could always furnish their house the way everyone else did—on the installment plan.

A surge in newspaper circulation—from 25 to 40 million daily between 1920 and 1930—gave everyone more to talk about. Captain Charles A. Lindbergh made the biggest headlines with his 1927 solo flight across the Atlantic in the single-engine *Spirit of St. Louis.* But he lost front page status in the same year to Babe Ruth's record-breaking 60 home runs. When John T. Scopes went on trial in Tennessee in 1925 for teaching evolution in the schools, readers followed every legal argument presented for and against by Clarence Darrow and William Jennings Bryan. The gossip columnists made intimates of the Prince of Wales, pilot Eddie Rickenbacker and financier Bernard Baruch. Albert Einstein and Sigmund Freud shared space with evangelists Billy Sunday and Aimee Semple McPherson. Flagpole sitters, dance marathon winners and rocking chair derby champions all had their moment of fame in the tabloids.

In their quest for features to feed the news-hungry public, reporters turned up a story in Hershey, Pennsylvania, that went back nearly 14 years. One full-page headline of 1923 read "Why

Hershey Gave $60,000,000 to Better the Lot of Orphans" and the lead sentence was Milton Hershey's simple explanation: "I was a poor boy myself, once." His own rise from hardship to wealth had prompted Hershey, in 1909, to found the Hershey Industrial School for boys who had lost one or both parents. The school began with a deed of 486 acres of farmland in Derry Township, an endowment of 500,000 shares of stock in the Hershey Chocolate Company and the arrival of two small fatherless boys, who moved into Hershey's childhood home, the Homestead. There they studied academic subjects and mastered practical skills. As enrollment grew, Hershey added land, buildings and teaching staff.

By 1923 Milton Hershey was "father" to 120 boys, aged four to 18, and they were heirs of Hershey Chocolate. When reporters probed for reasons why, Milton Hershey overcame his usual shyness to offer a brief bit of the philosophy behind his benevolence. "It is time," he said, "that more attention was paid to humanity and less to machinery; to polishing up men and not brass."

Milton Hershey and one of his "boys" in a reprint from the 1923 newspaper feature

Old-Fashioned Chocolate Soda

¼ cup club soda, chilled	2 scoops vanilla ice cream
3 tablespoons Hershey's	Additional club soda,
Chocolate Flavored Syrup	chilled

Combine ¼ cup club soda and chocolate syrup in tall glass (about 12 ounces); add scoops of ice cream. Fill glass with additional club soda; stir lightly. Garnish with whipped cream and cherry on top, if desired. *1 serving.*

Double Chocolate Soda: Use 2 scoops chocolate ice cream instead of vanilla ice cream.

Hershey's Chocoberry Splash

¾ cup low fat or skim milk	2 tablespoons Hershey's Chocolate Flavored Syrup
3 tablespoons frozen strawberries with syrup, thawed	2 tablespoons vanilla ice cream
	Splash of club soda

Fill glass with crushed ice. Measure ingredients except club soda into blender container. Blend at medium speed until smooth. Pour into glass over crushed ice. Splash in club soda; stir. Top with a scoop of vanilla ice cream and garnish with additional fruit, if desired. *1 serving.*

Flavor variations: Substitute the following fruit amounts for the strawberries:
Peach: ⅓ cup canned peach slices or 1 peach half
Raspberry: 3 tablespoons frozen raspberries with syrup, thawed
Pineapple: 2 slices canned or ¼ cup crushed pineapple
Fresh Strawberry: ¼ cup sweetened strawberries

Instant Shimmy Shake

3 cups milk	2 cups coffee ice cream, softened
⅔ cup Hershey's Instant	
1 teaspoon instant coffee granules	

Place all ingredients in blender container or mixer bowl. Blend at low speed until all ingredients are combined. *Three 12-ounce servings.*

Chocolate Instant Shimmy Shake: Place milk, Hershey's Instant and 2 cups vanilla ice cream in blender container or mixer bowl; blend at low speed until well combined.

(Top to bottom) Hershey's Chocoberry Splash, Instant Shimmy Shake, Charleston Hot Chocolate

Charleston Hot Chocolate

3 tablespoons sugar
2 tablespoons Hershey's
  Cocoa
2 tablespoons water
2 cups milk

¼ teaspoon vanilla
Whipped cream, non-dairy
  whipped topping or
  marshmallows

Combine sugar, cocoa and water in small saucepan. Bring to a boil over medium heat, stirring constantly. Add milk and heat to serving temperature. Do not boil. Add vanilla; serve in mugs and top with a spoonful of whipped cream, topping or marshmallows. *2 servings.*

Variations: If desired, add one of the following:
Banana: 1 mashed medium banana*
Mocha: 1 teaspoon instant coffee granules
Peanut Butter: ¼ cup creamy peanut butter*
Mint: 1 tablespoon crushed mint candy or ¼ teaspoon mint extract
Cinnamon: ¼ teaspoon ground cinnamon or cinnamon stick

*Best when combined with blender

Lucky Lindy Floats

2 cups cold milk
2 cups vanilla ice cream,
  softened

¾ cup Hershey's Chocolate
  Flavored Syrup

Place milk, 1 cup ice cream and chocolate syrup in blender container; cover. Blend on medium speed about 15 seconds or until smooth. Pour into 3 tall glasses and top with scoops of remaining ice cream. *Three 10-ounce servings.*

Flavor Variations: Add before blending:
Peanut Butter: 2 tablespoons creamy peanut butter
Cherry: ¼ cup maraschino cherry juice
Peach: ⅔ cup fresh or drained canned peach slices
Pineapple: 1 cup drained crushed pineapple
Mint: ½ teaspoon mint or peppermint extract

A Storage Hint

Hershey's Cocoa, Instant and Hot Cocoa Mix keep very well when stored at room temperature in tightly sealed containers. Store open cans of Hershey's Chocolate Flavored Syrup and Hershey's Fudge Topping in refrigerator. For more hints, turn to page 95.

Family Fun Cocoa

½ cup sugar
¼ cup Hershey's Cocoa
Dash salt (optional)

⅓ cup hot water
4 cups milk
¾ teaspoon vanilla

Combine sugar, cocoa and salt (if desired) in 1½-quart saucepan; blend in hot water. Bring to boil over medium heat, stirring constantly; boil and stir 2 minutes. Add milk; heat thoroughly. Stir occasionally; do not boil. Remove from heat; stir in vanilla. Serve hot. *About six 6-ounce servings.*

Jazz Age Eggnog

⅔ cup Hershey's Instant
¼ cup sugar
¼ teaspoon salt
4 egg yolks, slightly
   beaten
4 cups milk

3 to 4 tablespoons light
   rum or ¼ teaspoon rum
   extract
Chocolate Meringue
   (recipe below)
Ground nutmeg

Thoroughly combine Instant, sugar, salt and egg yolks in saucepan; gradually stir in 2 cups milk. Cook over medium heat, stirring constantly, until mixture just coats a spoon; do not boil. Add remaining 2 cups milk; heat to serving temperature. Remove from heat; add rum or extract. Carefully fold in Chocolate Meringue. Sprinkle individual servings with nutmeg. *Fourteen 4-ounce servings.*

Chocolate Meringue: Beat 4 egg whites and 2 tablespoons sugar in small bowl until stiff peaks form; gradually blend in 3 tablespoons Instant at low speed.

Variation: To serve cold Jazz Age Eggnog, remove cooked mixture from heat and add 2 cups milk; cool. Chill. Just before serving add rum or extract and fold in Chocolate Meringue.

The Flapper's Slimmer

2 tablespoons skim milk
1½ tablespoons brown
   sugar or equivalent
   sweetener

1 tablespoon Hershey's
   Cocoa
1 cup hot skim milk
⅛ teaspoon vanilla

Combine 2 tablespoons skim milk, brown sugar and cocoa in a mug or cup; blend well. Add remaining skim milk and vanilla. Stir to blend well. *1 serving.*

Variations: If desired, add one of the following:
Mocha: ½ teaspoon instant coffee granules
Cinnamon: dash cinnamon
Mint: 1 or 2 drops mint extract or 1 teaspoon crushed mint candy

the Thirties
the nation "goes bust," Hershey builds,
Hollywood dreams . . . and homemade
puddings and ice cream triumph!

By 1930, the stock market crash of October 29, 1929, had cast a long shadow across the United States. In two years, 25 percent of the labor force—more than 13 million people—were out of a job. Industrial output declined by half. Only one car was produced for every four made in 1929. "Hoovervilles," the shantytowns named for President Herbert Hoover elected in 1928, sprang up to shelter an estimated two million people who had lost their homes. In the big cities, people lined up at soup kitchens for something to eat; in the country, mortgages were foreclosed and farmers evicted.

The residents of Hershey must have been astounded by their good fortune. Throughout the decade-long Depression, nobody was laid off. In 1930, Milton Hershey saw all the omens of continuing hard times, and he decided to fend off the consequences in Derry Township. From a mix of kindness, business acumen and great courage, he conceived a plan to create jobs: he would take advantage of the low prices of building materials to construct six town landmarks.

After waving aside his associates' fears that the market for chocolate would fall, Hershey pulled out old architectural plans and commissioned new ones. He immediately set men to work digging the foundation for the first project, the Community Building, which, when completed in 1933, contained two theaters, a dining room and a cafeteria, as well as a gymnasium, swimming pool, bowling alley and photography room. While one crew was working on the Community Building, another was hurrying to complete the lavish, 170-room Hotel Hershey. And on November 15, 1934, the town's founder could celebrate the 25th anniversary of the Hershey Industrial

School by welcoming his 800 "adopted sons" to a huge, brand-new high school building.

In the fall of 1934, one fourth of the population of New York City was "on relief," dependent on public aid for survival. In 1938, there were still 10 million Americans out of work. But both construction and chocolate production continued in Hershey, where full wages were maintained and everyone had a job. By the end of the decade, the results of Milton Hershey's ambitious building program were evident in a handsome office building for the chocolate factory, a 16,000-seat stadium and the 7,200-seat Sports Arena, which was shaped entirely from reinforced concrete and considered an architectural wonder of its time.

Fred Astaire and Ginger
Rogers dance a new step
in the movie, Top Hat

President Franklin Delano Roosevelt

Nationwide, millions of hard-pressed voters placed their hopes in the "New Deal" promised by presidential candidate Franklin Delano Roosevelt in 1932. The economy would not revive enough during the thirties to put everyone back to work, but Roosevelt became one of America's most beloved presidents for the relief measures he was able to provide. The emblem of his National Recovery Administration was a blue eagle that came to symbolize popular support for a broad range of social programs, including the abolition of child labor and the funding of public jobs. Under Roosevelt's leadership, thousands of people went to work for the government, doing everything from building electric power plants and combating soil erosion by planting trees to performing in federally sponsored theaters and writing travel guides. When the president discussed his programs in radio "fireside chats," he won people's hearts with his reassuring, down-to-earth manner. And when his wife, Eleanor, traveled to coal mines, factories and towns devastated by the Depression, she won warm admiration for her brave humanitarianism.

People wanted to forget the times in which they lived. So they turned to the fairy tale world of Walt Disney's *Snow White and the Seven Dwarfs,* the first full-length animated film. They flocked to movie theaters to hear Judy Garland sing "Over the Rainbow" in *The Wizard of Oz,* and they were swept away by the ethereal dancing of Fred Astaire and Ginger Rogers. Shirley Temple bounced to fame during the thirties in *Little Miss Marker,* and Busby Berkeley mesmerized audiences with his celluloid world of music, chorus lines, money and success. While the machines of war were being mobilized in Europe, Hollywood was dampening hankies with the epic romance of *Gone With the Wind.* By the mid-thirties, 60 percent of all Americans went to the movies weekly. They might not have had much hope that prosperity was just around the corner, but they had every reason to dream.

Hotel Hershey, built during the Depression (and still standing today)

Top Hat Custard Ice Cream

1¾ cups sugar	3½ ounces Hershey's
¼ cup unsifted all-purpose	Unsweetened Baking
flour	Chocolate, broken
¼ teaspoon salt	into pieces
2 cups milk	4 cups light cream
2 eggs, slightly beaten	1 tablespoon vanilla

Combine sugar, flour and salt in a saucepan. Stir in milk; blend in eggs and add baking chocolate. Cook over medium heat, stirring constantly, until mixture thickens and begins to boil; boil 1 minute. Cool. Add light cream and vanilla to cooled custard. Fill chilled ice-cream container no more than ⅔ full. Freeze in ice-cream freezer according to manufacturer's directions. *About 2 quarts ice cream.*

Chocolate Rum Nut Ice Cream: Add 1 teaspoon rum extract instead of vanilla to cooled custard mixture. Saute ¾ cup coarsely chopped nuts in 2 tablespoons butter over medium heat for 3 minutes. Add nuts to partially frozen ice cream midway during freezing.

Dreamy Choco-Nut Ice Cream

⅓ cup Hershey's Cocoa	2 teaspoons vanilla
1 envelope unflavored	1 teaspoon almond extract
gelatine	1 cup chopped almonds
1 cup cold water	
2 cups light cream*	
1⅓ cups (14-ounce can)	
sweetened condensed milk	

Combine cocoa and gelatine in small saucepan; thoroughly blend in ½ cup cold water. Cook and stir over low heat until gelatine is dissolved. Remove from heat; add remaining ½ cup water. Blend in remaining ingredients except almonds. Freeze according to one of the following methods:

Refrigerator-freezer method: Pour chocolate mixture into 13 × 9-inch baking pan; cover and freeze to a firm mush (about 2 hours). Spoon into chilled, large mixer bowl; beat until smooth. Fold in almonds; cover and freeze until firm. *About 1½ quarts ice cream.*

Electric or crank-type freezer method: Add almonds to chocolate mixture; pour into ice cream freezer container. Freeze according to manufacturer's directions. *About 1½ quarts ice cream.*

Note: For 3-quart ice cream freezer double the preceding recipe.

*For extra rich cream: Use 1 cup heavy cream and 1 cup light cream instead of 2 cups light cream.

Top Hat Custard Ice Cream

Matinee Mint Parfaits

3 cups miniature or 30 large
   marshmallows
½ cup milk
1 cup Hershey's Semi-Sweet
   Chocolate Chips or
   Mini Chips

¼ cup confectioners' sugar
1½ cups heavy cream
2 tablespoons creme de
   menthe or ½ teaspoon
   mint extract plus 2
   drops green food color

Combine marshmallows and milk in saucepan; place over low heat and stir until marshmallows are melted and mixture is smooth. Pour 1 cup marshmallow mixture into small bowl; set aside. Add chocolate chips and confectioners' sugar to the remaining marshmallow mixture; return to low heat and stir until chips are melted. Remove from heat; cool to room temperature. Whip cream, fold 1½ cups into marshmallow mixture. Flavor with creme de menthe or mint extract and food color. Fold remaining whipped cream into chocolate mixture. Alternately spoon chocolate and mint mixtures into parfait glasses. Chill thoroughly or freeze. Garnish with candy mint leaves, if desired. *6 servings.*

Peppermint Variation: Substitute 2 tablespoons crushed peppermint candy; add 1 or 2 drops red food color, if desired.

Back Porch Chocolate Ice Cream

½ cup Hershey's Cocoa
¾ cup sugar
1 cup milk
3 egg yolks, slightly beaten

1 tablespoon vanilla
2 cups heavy cream
¼ cup sugar

Combine cocoa and ¾ cup sugar in small saucepan. Gradually blend in milk and egg yolks. Cook, stirring constantly, until mixture is very hot and thickens. Do not boil. Remove from heat; cool. Stir in vanilla. Freeze according to one of the following methods:

Refrigerator freezer method: Pour into refrigerator tray or 9-inch square pan. Freeze until slushy, about 1 hour. Whip cream in large mixer bowl; add ¼ cup sugar and beat until stiff. Spoon partially frozen chocolate mixture into small chilled mixer bowl; beat until smooth. Fold into whipped cream. Place bowl in freezer or pour into square pan. Freeze several hours until firm. Stir occasionally during first hour. *About 1½ quarts ice cream.*

Electric or crank-type freezer method: Stir in cream (unwhipped) and ¼ cup sugar. Fill ice cream container no more than ⅔ full. Freeze in ice-cream freezer according to manufacturer's directions.
About 1½ quarts ice cream.

Easy Chocolate Ice Cream

1⅓ cups (14-ounce can)
    sweetened condensed
    milk
⅔ cup Hershey's Chocolate
    Flavored Syrup

2 cups heavy cream,
    whipped

Stir together sweetened condensed milk and syrup in large bowl. Fold in whipped cream. Pour into aluminum foil-lined 9 × 5-inch loaf pan; cover. Freeze 6 hours or until firm. Scoop ice cream from pan or remove from pan, peel off foil and slice. Return leftovers to freezer. *About 1½ quarts.*

Blue Eagle Chocolate Bar Mousse

2 Hershey's Milk Chocolate
    Bars (½ pound each)
2 ounces Hershey's
    Unsweetened Baking
    Chocolate
5 tablespoons water
2 tablespoons rum or brandy

2 egg yolks
¼ cup butter
1 cup heavy cream
18 ladyfingers, split
4 egg whites
Chopped almonds
    (optional)

Break chocolate into pieces; combine milk chocolate and baking chocolate with water and rum or brandy in top of double boiler. Place over hot, not boiling, water and stir until melted and smooth. Remove from heat; blend in egg yolks. Add butter, a little at a time, stirring until blended. Whip cream; carefully fold into chocolate mixture. Chill 1 hour or until mixture begins to set. Meanwhile, line bottom and sides of an 8 or 9-inch springform pan with ladyfingers. Beat egg whites until stiff, but not dry. Carefully fold into chocolate mixture. Pour into lined mold and chill 8 hours or overnight. Garnish with chopped almonds, if desired. *14 to 16 servings.*

Swingtime Chocolate Mousse

3 ounces Hershey's
    Unsweetened Baking
    Chocolate
⅓ cup water
¾ cup sugar

⅛ teaspoon salt
3 egg yolks, well beaten
1 teaspoon vanilla
2 cups heavy cream

Combine baking chocolate and water in saucepan. Bring to boil over low heat, stirring vigorously, until blended. Add sugar and salt; simmer 3 minutes, stirring constantly. Pour mixture slowly over egg yolks, stirring well. Cool; add vanilla. Whip the cream until stiff; fold into chocolate mixture. Pour mixture into a refrigerator freezing tray and freeze 3 to 4 hours. *6 to 8 servings.*

Better-Times Chocolate Pudding

⅔ cup sugar
¼ cup Hershey's Cocoa
3 tablespoons cornstarch
¼ teaspoon salt

2¼ cups milk
2 tablespoons butter or
   margarine
1 teaspoon vanilla

Combine sugar, cocoa, cornstarch and salt in medium saucepan; gradually stir in milk. Cook over medium heat, stirring constantly, until mixture boils; boil and stir 1 minute. Remove from heat; blend in butter or margarine and vanilla. Pour into individual serving dishes. Carefully press plastic wrap onto surface. Chill. Garnish with whipped topping and chopped nuts, if desired. *4 to 5 servings.*

Big Apple Rum Souffle

2 envelopes unflavored
   gelatine
½ cup water
1¼ cups milk
6 egg yolks
3 tablespoons butter
2 teaspoons vanilla
6 egg whites
¼ teaspoon cream of tartar

⅓ cup sugar
1½ cups (1-pound can)
   Hershey's Chocolate
   Flavored Syrup
3 tablespoons rum or
   apple juice
1½ cups heavy cream
Chopped nuts or coconut
   cookie crumbs

Measure a length of aluminum foil to go around a 1-quart souffle dish; fold in half lengthwise. Lightly oil one side of collar or spray with natural vegetable spray. Tape securely to outside of dish (oiled side in) allowing collar to extend 4 inches above rim of dish.

Soften gelatine in water for 3 to 4 minutes in a medium saucepan. Combine milk and egg yolks; blend into softened gelatine. Add butter. Cook over medium heat, stirring constantly, until mixture *just* begins to boil. Remove from heat; blend in vanilla. Pour into large bowl; press plastic wrap onto surface. Cool; chill, stirring occasionally, until mixture mounds when dropped from a spoon.

Beat egg whites with cream of tartar in large mixer bowl until foamy; gradually add sugar, beating until stiff peaks form. Beat gelatine mixture in large mixer bowl on high speed just until smooth; blend in chocolate syrup and rum or apple juice. Fold chocolate mixture into beaten egg whites. Whip cream in small mixer bowl until stiff; fold into chocolate mixture, blending well. Pour into prepared dish; cover and chill overnight.

Just before serving, carefully remove foil collar. Gently pat nuts or cookie crumbs onto sides of souffle. Garnish top with chocolate curls, if desired. *12 to 14 servings.*

*(Top to bottom) Better-Times Chocolate Pudding,
Big Apple Rum Souffle, Fireside Steamed Pudding and
Cherry Whipped Cream, Movie Palace Eclairs*

Fireside Steamed Pudding

1½ cups dry bread crumbs	2 tablespoons butter, melted
¾ cup sugar	½ teaspoon almond extract
2 tablespoons unsifted all-purpose flour	¼ teaspoon red food color
½ teaspoon baking powder	7 egg whites
⅛ teaspoon salt	¼ cup sugar
6 egg yolks, slightly beaten	1 cup Hershey's Semi-Sweet Chocolate Mini Chips
2 cups (1 pound 6-ounce can) cherry pie filling	Cherry Whipped Cream (recipe below)

Combine bread crumbs, ¾ cup sugar, flour, baking powder and salt in a large bowl. Combine egg yolks, 1½ cups of the cherry pie filling, melted butter, almond extract and food color; thoroughly blend into crumb mixture. Beat egg whites until foamy; gradually add ¼ cup sugar and beat until stiff peaks form. Fold ⅓ beaten egg whites into cherry mixture, blending thoroughly. Fold in remaining egg whites; gently fold in Mini Chips. Pour batter into a well-greased 8-cup tube mold or heat-proof bowl. (If tube is open at top, cover with foil; grease foil.) Cover mold with wax paper and foil; tie securely with string. Place a rack in a large kettle; pour water into kettle to top of rack. Bring water to a boil; place mold on rack. Cover kettle and steam over simmering water about 1½ hours or until cake tester inserted comes out clean. (Additional water may be needed.) Remove from heat; cool in pan 5 minutes. Remove cover; unmold and serve warm with Cherry Whipped Cream. *12 to 14 servings.*

Cherry Whipped Cream: Beat 1 cup heavy cream with ¼ cup confectioners' sugar until stiff; fold in remaining cherry pie filling (about ½ cup) and ½ teaspoon almond extract.

Some Special Chocolate Decorations

Leaves: Gather 20 to 25 medium-size leaves with stems (English ivy, elm, dogwood). Wash and dry thoroughly. Melt 1 cup semi-sweet chocolate chips in top of double boiler over hot, not boiling, water. Remove from heat; keep pan over warm water. Carefully brush a thin layer (about 1/8-inch thick) of chocolate on the underside of each leaf. Chocolate and leaf will later separate more easily if the edges are not covered. Place coated leaves on wire rack until firm; chill if necessary. Carefully peel each leaf from the coating; store in cool place or refrigerator.

Curls: Draw the blade of a vegetable parer over the smooth side of a slightly warm block of unsweetened baking chocolate or a dark, sweet chocolate bar.

Movie Palace Eclairs

Eclair Filling
(recipe below)
1 cup water
½ cup butter or margarine
¼ teaspoon salt

1 cup unsifted all-purpose
flour
4 eggs
Eclair Glaze
(recipe below)

Prepare Eclair Filling; chill. Heat water, butter or margarine and salt to rolling boil in a saucepan. Add flour all at once; stir vigorously over low heat about 1 minute or until mixture leaves side of pan and forms a ball. Remove from heat; cool slightly. Add eggs, one at a time, beating until smooth and velvety. For eclairs, shape dough by scant ¼ cupfuls into fingers 4 inches long and 1 inch wide or drop scant ¼ cupfuls about 2 inches apart for puffs on ungreased baking sheet. Bake at 400°F for 35 to 40 minutes or until puffed and golden brown. While warm, horizontally slice off small portion of top. Remove any soft filaments of dough; cool. Prepare Eclair Glaze. Fill eclairs or puffs with Eclair Filling. Replace tops; glaze with Eclair Glaze or dust with confectioners' sugar. Chill. *12 eclairs or puffs.*

Eclair Filling

5 tablespoons cornstarch
¼ cup sugar
¼ teaspoon salt
3 cups milk

3 egg yolks, slightly beaten
1 teaspoon vanilla
1 Hershey's Milk Chocolate
Bar (½ pound)

Combine cornstarch, sugar, salt and milk in medium saucepan; blend in egg yolks. Cook over medium heat, stirring constantly, until mixture boils; boil and stir 1 minute. Remove from heat; add vanilla and chocolate bar, broken into pieces. Stir until chocolate is completely melted. Pour into bowl and press plastic wrap directly onto surface; cool. *About 4 cups filling.*

Eclair Glaze

4 ounces Hershey's Milk
Chocolate Bar

1 tablespoon water

Melt chocolate in water in top of double boiler over warm water; stir to blend well. (An additional teaspoon of water may be added if glaze is too thick.) *About ½ cup glaze.*

Note: If chocolate thickens and/or becomes grainy, add shortening, 1 teaspoon at a time, stirring until mixture becomes smooth.

the Forties

*World War II, the Home Front, radio's
Golden Age, victory's rewards . . . and
the taste of creamy chocolate pies*

Eighty-six percent of American households had acquired radios by 1940. So millions of people were enjoying their favorite broadcasts on Sunday, December 7, 1941, when announcers broke in with the shocking news: Japanese bombers had attacked Pearl Harbor. More than 2,400 Americans stationed at the Hawaiian Naval base had been killed, and over a thousand were wounded. The entire Pacific air fleet had been wiped out, and 18 ships had been damaged or sunk. President Franklin Delano Roosevelt called it "a day which will live in infamy" and asked for a declaration of war against Japan, Germany and Italy.

Thus America entered World War II. During the next four years, 15 million men and women served in the armed forces. Production of iron, steel, aluminum and other defense materials was increased dramatically. American troops fought all over the world, from Sicily to Burma, from the Sahara to the South Pacific, and more than 400,000 soldiers died. The landing of American troops at Normandy on June 6, 1944, was the mightiest military feat of its kind in modern history, and its success

anticipated Germany's surrender on May 8, 1945. Explosions of America's "secret weapon"—the atom bomb—in Hiroshima and Nagasaki, brought an end to bloodshed in the trans-Pacific war with Japan on August 14, 1945. It was a war unlike any other, and it had to be fought without precedents.

The home front reflected the demands of victory. Some 27 million people moved around the country as war-production industries sprang up in previously sleepy towns. There was no time to build housing; people slept on floors and shared beds. Gasoline, shoes, meat and coffee were rationed; hotel rooms, train seats and women's stockings were nearly impossible to obtain.

Children collected scrap metal, tended victory gardens and turned on the radio after school to hear the latest anti-Fascist blows struck by heroes Jack Armstrong and Superman. Their mothers went to work in munitions and aircraft plants, shipyards and offices; in the evening, they tuned in Lowell Thomas for the latest news from Tripoli, the Ardennes Forest, Okinawa, Guadalcanal and other far-off battlegrounds that held the whereabouts of fathers, husbands and sons.

War production in Hershey took the unique form of Field Ration D, a four-ounce chocolate bar that would not melt in a soldier's pocket and could provide a survival ration of 600 calories. The factory turned out 500,000 Ration D bars daily, its mission signaled by the Army-Navy "E" flag that flew outside as a special award for wartime efficiency.

*Milton Hershey accepts
the Army-Navy "E" flag
awarded to Hershey
employees in 1942*

Everyone worried and worked and waited. Some of the lonely hours could be passed in movie theaters, but Hollywood's offerings did not bring forgetfulness. The reminders ranged from the suspense of *Thirty Seconds Over Tokyo* to the poignant liaison of Humphrey Bogart and Ingrid Bergman in *Casablanca*. Charlie Chaplin mocked Nazism in *The Great Dictator*, and Donald Duck quacked at fear in *Der Fuehrer's Face*. Bugs Bunny rose to the cause of *Herr Meets Hare*, but audiences sympathized more with *The Story of G.I. Joe*. Audiences were roused by the patriotism of James Cagney in *Yankee Doodle Dandy* and were reassured by Bing Crosby's gentle performance in *Going My Way*.

Laughter that broke the wartime tension came regularly when "The Jack Benny Program" was on the air. Audiences roared everytime Jack Benny paused; his violin lessons were not to be missed. Listeners stayed tuned for Fred Allen's brilliant wit and his visits with the legendary denizens of Allen's Alley. Other stars that made the forties

the "Golden Age of Radio" were a sassy blockhead called Charlie McCarthy; a big-nosed banterer known both as Jimmy Durante and "the Schnozz"; and a skinny young singer named Frank Sinatra, who broke in with the big-band sounds of Tommy Dorsey's orchestra. Television was a pre-war invention, but it didn't reach consumers until after the troops came home.

In Pennsylvania, Milton Hershey lived to see the victory but not the rewards of the decade, for he died on October 13, 1945, at the age of 88. By the end of 1945, America turned its enormous wartime industrial capacity to peacetime uses. Four million new homes, 19.5 million cars and trucks, synthetic fibers and antibiotics yielded higher standards of living and greater expectations of health and well-being. Almost one and a half million college degrees were awarded between 1945 and 1950, as G.I.'s and factory veterans pursued opportunities offered by peace. And across the country—from post-war promises kept and households resumed—30 million babies were born.

Elegant Chocolate Mousse Pie

9-inch Graham Crumb
Crust (recipe below)
¾ cup sweet butter
¾ cup Hershey's Cocoa
3 eggs, separated
¼ cup sugar

¼ cup heavy cream
3 tablespoons orange liqueur
  or rum
½ cup sugar
¾ cup heavy cream
2 teaspoons vanilla

Prepare crumb crust; set aside. Melt butter in saucepan. Remove from heat; completely blend in cocoa. Cool to room temperature. Beat egg yolks in small mixer bowl; gradually add ¼ cup sugar, beating until thick and lemon colored. Blend in chocolate mixture, ¼ cup heavy cream and liqueur; set aside.

Beat egg whites until foamy; gradually add ½ cup sugar, beating until stiff peaks form. Fold into chocolate mixture. Beat ¾ cup heavy cream with vanilla until stiff; gently fold into chocolate mixture. Spoon into pie shell; chill several hours. Garnish with additional whipped cream and chocolate shavings, if desired. *8 to 10 servings.*

Graham Crumb Crust: Combine 1¼ cups graham cracker crumbs, ¼ cup sugar and ¼ cup melted butter or margarine. Press crumb mixture onto bottom and up sides of a 9-inch pie pan. Bake at 375°F for 8 minutes; cool.

Classic Chocolate Cream Pie

9-inch baked pastry shell
  or crumb crust, cooled
2½ ounces Hershey's
  Unsweetened Baking
  Chocolate
3 cups milk
1⅓ cups sugar

3 tablespoons unsifted
  all-purpose flour
3 tablespoons cornstarch
½ teaspoon salt
3 egg yolks
2 tablespoons butter
1½ teaspoons vanilla

Prepare pie shell; set aside. Melt baking chocolate with 2 cups milk in saucepan over medium heat, stirring constantly. Cook and stir *just* until mixture boils; remove from heat. Combine sugar, flour, cornstarch and salt. Blend egg yolks with remaining 1 cup milk; add to dry ingredients. Blend into chocolate mixture in saucepan. Cook over medium heat, stirring constantly, until mixture boils; boil and stir 1 minute. Remove from heat; add butter and vanilla. Pour into prepared pie shell; press plastic wrap onto filling. Cool; chill. Serve topped with sweetened whipped cream, if desired. *8 to 10 servings.*

Elegant Chocolate Mousse Pie

Big Band Black Bottom Pie

9-inch baked pastry shell
 or crumb crust, cooled
½ cup sugar
⅓ cup Hershey's Cocoa
¼ cup butter
1 envelope unflavored
 gelatine
¼ cup cold water

½ cup sugar
¼ cup cornstarch
2 cups milk
4 eggs, separated
1 teaspoon vanilla
2 tablespoons rum
½ cup sugar

Prepare pie shell; set aside. Combine ½ cup sugar, cocoa and butter in medium bowl; set aside. Combine gelatine and cold water in small bowl; place bowl in pan of simmering water to dissolve gelatine.

Mix ½ cup sugar, cornstarch, milk and egg yolks in saucepan. Cook over medium heat, stirring constantly, until mixture boils. Boil and stir 1 minute. Remove from heat; blend 1½ cups of custard into cocoa/sugar mixture. Add vanilla and pour into prepared pie shell; chill. Combine dissolved gelatine with remaining custard; add rum and set aside.

Beat egg whites until foamy; gradually add ½ cup sugar. Continue to beat until stiff peaks form. Fold gelatine/custard mixture into beaten egg whites. Chill 15 minutes or until partially set. Spoon over chocolate custard in pie shell. Chill. Garnish with chocolate curls or shavings before serving, if desired. *8 to 10 servings.*

Chattanooga Choo-Choo Pie

9-inch unbaked pastry shell
¼ teaspoon baking soda
1⅓ cups boiling water
1½ cups (1-pound can)
 Hershey's Chocolate
 Flavored Syrup
1 teaspoon vanilla

1⅓ cups unsifted all-purpose
 flour
½ cup sugar
¼ teaspoon baking soda
¼ teaspoon salt
⅓ cup butter or margarine
 Cinnamon

Prepare unbaked pastry shell; set aside. Dissolve ¼ teaspoon baking soda in boiling water; stir in chocolate syrup and vanilla. Set aside. Combine flour, sugar, ¼ teaspoon baking soda and salt; cut in butter or margarine to form coarse crumbs.

Set aside 1 cup each of chocolate mixture and crumbs; gently combine remaining chocolate and crumbs, stirring just until crumbs are moistened (mixture will be lumpy). Pour reserved 1 cup chocolate mixture into unbaked pastry shell; pour chocolate-crumb mixture evenly over liquid in shell. Sprinkle with remaining 1 cup crumbs and cinnamon. Bake at 375°F for 60 minutes; cool completely.
8 servings.

(Top to bottom) Big Band Black Bottom Pie, Chattanooga Choo-Choo Pie, Home Front Coconut Cream Pie

Home Front Coconut Cream Pie

9-inch baked pastry shell or crumb crust, cooled	½ cup flaked coconut
⅔ cup sugar	3 tablespoons Hershey's Cocoa
⅓ cup cornstarch	3 tablespoons sugar
¼ teaspoon salt	2 tablespoons milk
3 cups milk	3 egg whites
3 egg yolks, slightly beaten	¼ teaspoon cream of tartar
1 tablespoon butter	6 tablespoons sugar
2 teaspoons vanilla	

Prepare pie shell; set aside. Combine ⅔ cup sugar, cornstarch, salt and 3 cups milk in medium saucepan; blend in egg yolks. Cook over medium heat, stirring constantly, until mixture boils. Boil and stir one minute. Remove from heat; stir in butter and vanilla. Pour 1½ cups cream filling into a small bowl; stir in coconut. Set aside.

Combine cocoa, 3 tablespoons sugar and 2 tablespoons milk in a small bowl; blend into remaining cream filling in saucepan. Return to heat and bring just to a boil, stirring constantly. Remove from heat and pour 1 cup chocolate filling into pie shell. Spread coconut filling over chocolate layer. Top with remaining chocolate filling; spread evenly. Prepare meringue by beating egg whites with cream of tartar until foamy. Gradually add 6 tablespoons sugar; beat until stiff peaks form. Spread meringue onto hot pie filling; carefully sealing meringue to edge of crust. Bake at 350°F for 8 to 10 minutes or until lightly brown. Cool to room temperature; chill several hours.
8 to 10 servings.

D-Day Hershey Bar Pie

9-inch Chocolate Crumb Crust (recipe below)	⅓ cup milk
1 Hershey's Milk Chocolate Bar or Milk Chocolate Bar with Almonds (½ pound)	1½ cups miniature or 15 regular marshmallows
	1 cup heavy cream

Prepare crumb crust; set aside. Break bar, chopping almonds into small pieces; melt with milk and marshmallows in top of double boiler over hot, not boiling, water. Cool to room temperature. Whip cream until stiff; fold into chocolate mixture. Pour into crust; chill several hours until firm. Garnish with whipped topping or chilled cherry pie filling, if desired. *8 servings.*

Chocolate Crumb Crust: Combine 1½ cups vanilla wafer crumbs, 6 tablespoons Hershey's Cocoa, ⅓ cup confectioners' sugar and 6 tablespoons melted butter or margarine; press evenly onto bottom and up sides of a 9-inch pie pan. Bake at 350°F for 10 minutes; cool.

Crooner Cordial Pie

30 large or 3 cups miniature marshmallows	1 to 2 tablespoons creme de cacao
½ cup milk	5 cups (12-ounce container) frozen non-dairy whipped topping, thawed
1 cup Hershey's Semi-Sweet Chocolate Mini Chips	
1 teaspoon vanilla	9-inch Crumb Crust
1 to 2 tablespoons brandy	(recipe below)

Combine marshmallows and milk in saucepan; cook and stir over low heat until marshmallows are melted and mixture is smooth. Pour about 1 cup marshmallow mixture into a small bowl; set aside. Add Mini Chips to the remaining marshmallow mixture; return to low heat and stir until chips are melted. Remove from heat and stir in vanilla; cool to room temperature.

Stir brandy and creme de cacao into reserved marshmallow mixture; chill until mixture mounds slightly when dropped from a spoon (about 1 hour). Prepare Crumb Crust.

Fold 3 cups whipped topping into cooled chocolate mixture; spoon into cooled crumb crust. Blend remaining whipped topping into chilled brandy mixture; spread over chocolate mixture. Chill thoroughly until firm, about 2 hours. *8 to 10 servings.*

Crumb Crust: Combine 1¾ cups vanilla wafer crumbs, 3 tablespoons sugar and 6 tablespoons melted butter or margarine; press evenly onto bottom and up sides of a 9-inch pie pan. Bake at 350°F for 8 to 10 minutes; cool.

Substitution Hints

For baking chocolate: 3 tablespoons cocoa and 1 tablespoon shortening or oil equals 1 square (1 ounce) baking chocolate.

For pre-melted unsweetened chocolate: 3 tablespoons cocoa and 1 tablespoon oil or melted shortening equals 1 envelope (1 ounce) pre-melted unsweetened chocolate.

For semi-sweet chocolate: 6 tablespoons cocoa, 7 tablespoons sugar and ¼ cup shortening equals one 6-ounce package (1 cup) semi-sweet chocolate chips or 6 squares (1 ounce each) semi-sweet chocolate.

For sweet cooking chocolate: 3 tablespoons cocoa, 4½ tablespoons sugar and 2⅔ tablespoons shortening equals one 4-ounce bar sweet cooking chocolate.

Note: If you must substitute, don't use butter or margarine. Butter and margarine contain a slight amount of water that could cause ingredients to separate. See page 56 for other substitution hints.

Other Substitution Hints

There are three easy ways to blend cocoa into recipes that originally called for another chocolate product:

1) Combine cocoa (and sugar) with the dry ingredients. Add the extra shortening to the shortening already called for in the recipe.

2) Melt the extra shortening. Remove it from the heat and blend in cocoa. If you're using oil, of course no melting is necessary— merely blend oil and cocoa. Either way, add the mixture to the recipe as you would add pre-melted unsweetened chocolate.

3) Something special: for extra cocoa flavor and color, add the extra shortening to the shortening already called for in the recipe. Mix cocoa and part of the water in the recipe into a smooth paste, then add this to the creamed mixture.

Our Gal Sundae Pie

9-inch Macaroon-Nut
  Crust (recipe below)
⅔ cup packed light brown
  sugar
3 tablespoons unsifted
  all-purpose flour
2 tablespoons cornstarch
½ teaspoon salt

2¼ cups milk
½ cup (5.5-ounce can)
  Hershey's Chocolate
  Flavored Syrup
3 egg yolks, well beaten
2 tablespoons butter or
  margarine
1 teaspoon vanilla

Prepare crust; set aside. Combine brown sugar, flour, cornstarch and salt in a saucepan. Blend in milk, chocolate syrup and egg yolks. Cook over medium heat, stirring constantly, until mixture boils; boil and stir 1 minute. Remove from heat; blend in butter or margarine and vanilla. Pour into baked pie crust; place plastic wrap directly onto surface. Cool; chill. Serve with dollops of sweetened whipped cream, and if desired, garnish with maraschino cherries and squares of a Hershey's Milk Chocolate Bar. *8 servings.*

Macaroon-Nut Crust

1¼ cups coconut macaroon
  cookie crumbs
½ cup chopped walnuts

¼ cup butter or margarine,
  melted

Combine crumbs, walnuts and butter or margarine. Press firmly onto bottom and up sides of a 9-inch pie pan. Bake at 350°F for 8 to 10 minutes. Cool.

The Fifties

*coonskin caps, soaring tail fins, TV
sit-coms, rock and roll . . . and
luscious chocolate cakes*

In 1952, the genial smile of General Dwight D. Eisenhower seemed to signal that all would be well. Peace would be renewed after the withdrawal of American troops from Korea, and people could retreat from Cold War bomb fears to the pleasures of backyard barbecues. Voters ushered the World War II hero into office with big "I Like Ike" buttons, and their faith was not proved wrong. The peace and prosperity of the Eisenhower years, while not unblemished by crises and recession, did afford Americans more time and money for fun and frivolity than they had ever before enjoyed.

The decade became known for quiet conformity, but some of the sights of people at play were strange, indeed. In 1954, the streets of suburbia were invaded by an army of pint-sized frontiersmen waving the tails of their coonskin caps and toting Davy Crockett lunch boxes. Four years later, 30 million children dedicated their energies to the task of keeping plastic Hula-Hoops spinning around their waists. Grown men invested considerable elbow grease in the polishing challenge posed by the soaring tail fins of their two-tone sedans. Women deliberated the relative flattery of yard-wide crinolines and tapered "sack" dresses, short shorts and pedal pushers, pony tails and "poodle-cut" curls. At dinner time, the whole family would gladly abandon the convenience of their modern kitchen for the pre-historic smell of steaks and burgers burning on the grill. No doubt people worked hard in the fifties for the means to buy pop-it beads, Bermuda shorts and paint-by-number sets. But by 1959 they were spending fewer hours at work than in front of their 50 million television sets.

Television changed people's lives. In pre-tube days, sixty-three percent of the population was asleep by midnight, but once they were given the chance, seventy-five percent stayed up to watch Jack Parr, Jerry Lester and Steve Allen. Movie theaters lost half of their weekly attendance to the belly-laugh entertainment of Milton Berle, Sid Caesar and *I Love Lucy.* When the movies made a dramatic ef-

The classic 1957 Chevrolet—popular then and now

fort to lure viewers back, the result was even more bizarre than duck-tail haircuts and quiz-show scandals: theater seats quickly (and, alas, temporarily) filled with viewers eager to follow the adventure of *Bwana Devil* through special 3-D goggles. A more effective antidote to TV was the summernight lure of drive-in movies, where James Dean, Marlon Brando, Natalie Wood, Marilyn Monroe, Audrey Hepburn, Doris Day and Rock Hudson played to acres of parked cars hooked up for sound.

Oddly enough, the stars who did the most to change the landscape of American entertainment were members of the United States Senate. Millions of people rushed out to buy their first TV set when Senator Estes Kefauver and the Special Committee to Investigate Organized Crime subpoenaed gangsters to testify in front of TV cameras. In 1954, another wave of civic-minded

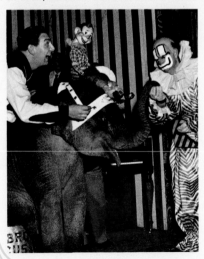

TV's *Buffalo Bob Smith, Howdy Doody* and *Clarabelle Clown*

TV watchers followed the proceedings of a government subcommittee assigned to investigate the charges of treason hurled by Senator Joseph McCarthy against the United States Army. Twenty million people saw Army counsel Joseph Welch weep at the Senator's insinuations; then they held their breath as Welch rose in anger to demand, "Have you no sense of decency, sir. . . .Have you left no sense of decency?" The question was resolved by the Senate, which voted to censure McCarthy.

The question of decency was aired again on TV in 1956—but in an entirely different context. The adversaries were rock-star Elvis Presley, who had taken the nation by storm with "Don't Be Cruel," and TV's top impresario, Ed Sullivan, who declared that he would never allow Presley's hips to swivel on his show. Eventually, they compromised: Presley bellowed "Hound Dog" for his legion of fans while Sullivan's crew filmed only half of Presley's image— from the waist up! But such cautiousness didn't stop the sound turnaround led by Elvis. By 1958, teenagers were buying seventy percent of all records sold, and as far as they were concerned, rock and roll was here to stay.

To be young in the late fifties was to learn how to do the "slop" from the fleet-footed regulars on *American Bandstand*, to dance the "lindy" in stockinged feet with Danny and the Juniors "At the Hop" and to identify readily with Dion's high-pitched complaint about being "A Teenager in Love." Rock and roll confirmed a natural consequence of the post-World War II baby boom: by the end of the fifties, a significant segment of America was reaching adolescence. From then on, as millions of households discovered, life would only get noisier!

Pink Flamingo Cake Roll

3 egg yolks
½ cup sugar
½ cup unsifted all-purpose
 flour
⅓ cup Hershey's Cocoa
⅓ cup sugar
½ teaspoon baking soda
¼ teaspoon salt

⅓ cup water
1 teaspoon vanilla
3 egg whites
1 tablespoon sugar
Strawberry Whipped
 Cream Filling and Frosting
 (recipe below)
Whole strawberries

Line a 15½ × 10½ × 1-inch jelly roll pan with aluminum foil; grease foil generously. Beat egg yolks about 3 minutes on high speed in small mixer bowl. Gradually add ½ cup sugar; continue beating for 2 minutes. Combine flour, cocoa, ⅓ cup sugar, baking soda and salt in small bowl; add alternately with water and vanilla on low speed just until batter is smooth. Beat egg whites until foamy; add 1 tablespoon sugar and beat until stiff peaks form. Carefully fold beaten egg whites into chocolate mixture. Spread batter evenly into prepared pan. Bake at 375°F for 15 to 18 minutes or until top springs back when touched lightly. Invert onto slightly dampened towel; carefully remove foil. Immediately roll cake and towel together from narrow end. Let stand 1 minute. Unroll and remove towel; reroll cake. Cool completely on wire rack. Prepare Strawberry Whipped Cream Filling and Frosting.

Unroll cake and spread with about 5 cups Strawberry Whipped Cream; reroll. Frost with remaining Strawberry Whipped Cream and garnish with whole strawberries. Chill about 1 hour before serving. *10 to 12 servings.*

Strawberry Whipped Cream Filling and Frosting

2 cups heavy cream
¾ cup confectioners' sugar
1 teaspoon vanilla

3 cups sliced strawberries,
 well drained (1 quart fresh
 or one 16-ounce package
 whole strawberries)

Beat heavy cream, confectioners' sugar and vanilla on high speed in mixer bowl until stiff. Fold sliced strawberries into whipped cream.

When is a Cake Done?

Ovens vary. Yours may be "slow" or "fast." So set your timer for the minimum time given in the recipe. When the timer rings, test by inserting a cake tester or toothpick into the center of the cake. If the tester comes out clean, your cake is done. Otherwise, more time is obviously needed.

Pink Flamingo Cake Roll

Chantilly Lace Chiffon Cake

⅔ cup Hershey's Cocoa	1 teaspoon salt
¾ cup boiling water	½ cup vegetable oil
7 egg whites	7 egg yolks
½ teaspoon cream of tartar	2 teaspoons vanilla
¼ cup sugar	Coconut Creme Filling
1½ cups unsifted cake flour	(recipe below)
1½ cups sugar	Cocoa Glaze
1½ teaspoons baking soda	(recipe below)

Stir together cocoa and boiling water in small bowl until smooth; set aside. Beat egg whites and cream of tartar in large mixer bowl until foamy; gradually add ¼ cup sugar and beat until stiff peaks form. Combine flour, 1½ cups sugar, baking soda and salt in large mixer bowl. Blend in oil, egg yolks, vanilla and reserved cocoa mixture on low speed until smooth. Fold about ¼ of beaten egg whites into chocolate mixture until thoroughly blended. Gently fold in remaining egg whites. Pour batter into an ungreased 10-inch tube pan. Bake at 325°F for 1 hour and 10 minutes or until top springs back when touched lightly. Invert until cool; remove from pan. Place cake on serving plate. Cut a ¾-inch layer from top; set aside. Cut around cake 1 inch from outer edge to 1 inch from bottom. Then cut around cake 1 inch from inner edge to 1 inch from bottom. Carefully remove cake between the cuts. Fill cavity with Coconut Creme Filling; place reserved cake layer on top. Pour Cocoa Glaze on top of cake and allow to drizzle down sides. *12 to 14 servings.*

Coconut Creme Filling

½ cup unsifted all-purpose	1 tablespoon vanilla
flour	¼ teaspoon salt
1 cup milk	2⅔ cups confectioners' sugar
½ cup butter or margarine	1⅓ cups (3½-ounce can)
½ cup shortening	flaked coconut

Combine flour and milk in a saucepan. Cook, stirring constantly, until mixture thickens and boils; boil and stir 1 minute. Cool. Cream butter or margarine and shortening in small mixer bowl. Add vanilla and salt; gradually add confectioners' sugar. Blend in cooled flour mixture and coconut. *About 4 cups filling.*

Cocoa Glaze: Combine ⅓ cup Hershey's Cocoa, 3 tablespoons melted butter or margarine and 2 tablespoons light corn syrup in small bowl; blend in 2 cups confectioners' sugar and 1 tablespoon vanilla. Add 4 to 5 tablespoons boiling water, one tablespoon at a time, until glaze is smooth and of pouring consistency. *About 1⅓ cups glaze.*

Sing-Along Swirl Cake

1 cup butter or margarine
2 cups sugar
1 teaspoon vanilla
5 eggs
2½ cups unsifted all-purpose
  flour
¾ teaspoon baking soda
¼ teaspoon salt
1½ cups sour cream

¼ cup honey or light corn
  syrup
¾ cup chopped pecans
1 Hershey's Milk Chocolate
  Bar (½ pound)
½ cup (5.5-ounce can)
  Hershey's Chocolate
  Flavored Syrup

Cream butter or margarine, sugar and vanilla in large mixer bowl until light and fluffy; add eggs and beat well. Combine flour, baking soda and salt; add alternately with sour cream to creamed mixture. Stir honey or corn syrup and pecans into 2 cups of batter; set aside. Melt chocolate bar in chocolate syrup over warm water; blend into remaining batter. Pour into a greased and floured 10-inch tube pan. Spoon reserved pecan mixture evenly over chocolate batter. Bake on lowest rack of oven at 350°F for 45 minutes; without opening oven door, decrease temperature to 325°F and continue to bake for 50 to 55 minutes or until cake tester inserted comes out clean. Cool cake one hour; remove from pan and cool completely. Glaze as desired. *12 to 14 servings.*

Fan Club Fudge Cake

2½ ounces Hershey's
  Unsweetened Baking
  Chocolate
¾ cup butter or margarine
2 cups sugar
2 eggs

1 teaspoon vanilla
2¼ cups unsifted all-purpose
  flour
1¼ teaspoons baking soda
½ teaspoon salt
1⅓ cups water

Melt baking chocolate in top of double boiler over hot, not boiling, water; cool slightly. Cream butter or margarine and sugar in large mixer bowl. Add eggs, vanilla and baking chocolate; blend well. Combine flour, baking soda and salt; add alternately with water to creamed mixture. Pour into two greased and floured 9-inch layer pans; bake at 350°F for 35 to 40 minutes or until cake tester inserted comes out clean. Cool 10 minutes; remove from pans. Cool completely; frost as desired. *8 to 10 servings.*

Pony Tail Pound Cake

1 cup butter or margarine	2 teaspoons baking powder
2 cups sugar	½ teaspoon salt
1½ teaspoons vanilla	1 cup milk
3 eggs	2 cups (12-ounce package)
3 cups unsifted all-purpose flour	Hershey's Semi-Sweet Chocolate Mini Chips

Cream butter or margarine, sugar and vanilla in a large mixer bowl until light and fluffy. Add eggs, one at a time, beating well after each addition. Combine flour, baking powder and salt; add alternately with milk to creamed mixture, beating just until smooth. Stir in Mini Chips. Pour into a well-greased and floured 12-cup Bundt pan or 10-inch tube pan. Bake at 350°F for 1 hour or until cake tester inserted comes out clean; cool completely. Remove from pan; sprinkle with confectioners' sugar or glaze as desired. *12 to 14 servings.*

Flying Saucer Crater Cake

Topping (recipe below)	1½ cups sugar
⅓ cup butter or margarine	1½ teaspoons baking soda
4 ounces Hershey's Unsweetened Baking Chocolate	1 teaspoon salt
	1½ cups sour cream
	2 eggs
1¾ cups unsifted all-purpose flour	1 teaspoon vanilla
	½ cup chopped nuts

Prepare Topping; set aside. Melt butter or margarine in small saucepan. Add baking chocolate and stir constantly over *low heat* until melted. Combine remaining ingredients except nuts in large mixer bowl. Blend in melted chocolate mixture; beat 3 minutes at medium speed. Pour into greased and floured 13 × 9 × 2-inch pan. Place half teaspoonful of Topping 1-inch apart on top of batter. With fork, streak Topping lightly over batter. Sprinkle with nuts. Bake at 350°F for 30 to 35 minutes or until cake tester inserted comes out clean. Cool. *12 to 14 servings.*

Topping

2 tablespoons butter or margarine	⅔ cup confectioners' sugar
1 ounce Hershey's Unsweetened Baking Chocolate	1 tablespoon milk
	¼ teaspoon vanilla

Melt butter or margarine in small saucepan; add baking chocolate and stir constantly over *very low heat* until melted. Blend confectioners' sugar, milk and vanilla in small mixer bowl until smooth. Add chocolate mixture; beat at high speed for 2 minutes. Set aside.

Drive-In Snack Cake

1¾ cups unsifted all-purpose flour	⅔ cup butter or margarine, softened
1¾ cups sugar	1½ cups sour cream
¾ cup Hershey's Cocoa	2 eggs
1½ teaspoons baking soda	1 teaspoon vanilla
1 teaspoon salt	

Combine flour, sugar, cocoa, baking soda and salt in large mixer bowl. Blend in butter or margarine, sour cream, eggs and vanilla on low speed. Beat 3 minutes on medium speed. Pour batter into greased and floured 13 × 9 × 2-inch pan. Bake at 350°F for 40 to 45 minutes or until cake tester inserted comes out clean. Cool completely; frost as desired. *12 to 14 servings.*

3-D Cheesecake

9-inch Crumb Crust (recipe below)	3 tablespoons unsifted all-purpose flour
1 cup Hershey's Semi-Sweet Chocolate Chips or Mini Chips	2 teaspoons vanilla
	½ cup sour cream (optional)
3 packages (8 ounces each) cream cheese, softened	1 tablespoon sugar (optional)
1 cup sugar	Cherry pie filling or sweetened strawberries (optional)
3 eggs	
½ cup sour cream	

Prepare Crumb Crust; refrigerate. Melt chocolate chips in top of double boiler over hot, not boiling, water. Set aside over warm water. Beat cream cheese and sugar in large mixer bowl until smooth and creamy. Blend in eggs. Gradually pour in chocolate mixture beating on low speed until well blended. Add ½ cup sour cream, flour and vanilla; blend until smooth. Pour into prepared crust; bake at 350°F for 55 to 60 minutes or until filling is firm. Turn oven off; cool cheesecake 1 hour without opening door. Cool completely. Chill several hours or overnight. Garnish just before serving with sweetened sour cream (if desired) made by combining 1 tablespoon sugar with ½ cup sour cream. Top with cherry pie filling or sweetened strawberries (if desired.) *12 to 14 servings.*

Crumb Crust

2 cups graham cracker or vanilla wafer crumbs	⅓ cup butter or margarine, melted
2 tablespoons sugar	

Combine crumbs, sugar and butter or margarine; press mixture into bottom and 2 inches up side of a 9-inch springform pan.

Pedal Pushers Upside-Down Cake

2 cups (1 pound 6-ounce can) cherry pie filling	1 teaspoon baking soda
1⅔ cups unsifted all-purpose flour	½ teaspoon salt
	1 cup water
1 cup sugar	⅓ cup vegetable oil
¼ cup Hershey's Cocoa	1 teaspoon vinegar
	½ teaspoon vanilla

Spread cherry pie filling evenly in bottom of an ungreased 9-inch square cake pan; set aside. Combine flour, sugar, cocoa, baking soda and salt in mixing bowl. Add water, oil, vinegar and vanilla; stir until batter is smooth and well blended. Pour evenly onto cherries in pan. Bake at 350°F for 40 to 45 minutes or until cake tester inserted comes out clean. Immediately invert onto serving plate. Serve warm or cold with sweetened whipped cream, if desired. *8 to 10 servings.*

Two-Tone Cup Cakes

Mini Chip Filling (recipe below)	1 teaspoon baking soda
	½ teaspoon salt
1½ cups unsifted all-purpose flour	⅓ cup vegetable oil
	1 cup water
1 cup sugar	1 tablespoon vinegar
⅓ cup Hershey's Cocoa	1 teaspoon vanilla

Prepare filling; set aside. Combine remaining ingredients in order listed in a large mixer bowl; blend on low speed until well mixed. Fill paper-lined muffin cups (2½ inches in diameter) ½ full with batter. Spoon about 1 tablespoon filling onto each cupcake. Bake at 350°F for 20 to 25 minutes or until toothpick inserted in cake portion comes out clean. *About 24 cupcakes.*

Orange Variation: Add 2 teaspoons grated orange peel and 3 or 4 drops orange food color to filling ingredients.

Mini Chip Filling

1 package (8 ounces) cream cheese	⅛ teaspoon salt
⅓ cup sugar	1 cup Hershey's Semi-Sweet Chocolate Mini Chips
1 egg	

Combine cream cheese, sugar, egg and salt in a mixing bowl; beat until smooth. Add Mini Chips; set aside.

Pedal Pushers Upside-Down Cake

Bridge Party Coffee Cake

1 cup butter or margarine, softened	1 teaspoon baking powder
2 cups sugar	¼ teaspoon salt
2 eggs	1 cup chopped nuts
1 cup sour cream	½ cup shredded coconut
1 teaspoon grated lemon peel	¼ cup Hershey's Cocoa
1 teaspoon lemon juice	¼ cup sugar
2 cups unsifted all-purpose flour	1 teaspoon cinnamon
	2 tablespoons butter or margarine, melted

Cream 1 cup butter or margarine, 2 cups sugar and eggs in large mixer bowl. Blend in sour cream, lemon peel and juice. Combine flour, baking powder and salt; blend into creamed mixture. Combine nuts, coconut, cocoa, ¼ cup sugar and cinnamon in small bowl; add melted butter or margarine. Set aside. Spoon half of batter into greased and floured 12-cup Bundt pan or 10-inch tube pan. Sprinkle with half of nut mixture. Top with remaining batter and nut mixture. Bake at 350°F for 60 minutes or until cake tester inserted comes out clean. Cool 10 minutes; remove from pan. Cool completely; sprinkle with confectioners' sugar, if desired. *12 to 14 servings.*

April Love Pecan Cake

½ cup Hershey's Cocoa	1½ teaspoons baking soda
½ cup boiling water	1 cup buttermilk or sour milk*
¼ cup butter or margarine	
¼ cup shortening	1¾ cups unsifted all-purpose flour
2 cups sugar	
⅛ teaspoon salt	3 tablespoons buttermilk or sour milk**
1 teaspoon vanilla	
2 eggs	⅓ cup chopped pecans

Stir together cocoa and boiling water in small bowl until smooth; set aside. Cream butter or margarine, shortening, sugar, salt and vanilla in large mixer bowl. Add eggs; beat well. Stir baking soda into 1 cup buttermilk or sour milk; add alternately with flour to creamed mixture. Measure 1⅔ cups batter into small bowl. Stir in 3 tablespoons buttermilk or sour milk and pecans; pour into a greased and wax paper-lined 8 or 9-inch layer pan. Blend cocoa mixture into remaining batter; pour into two greased and wax paper-lined 8 or 9-inch layer pans. Bake at 350°F for 30 to 35 minutes for 8-inch layers; 25 to 30 minutes for 9-inch layers or until cake tester inserted comes out clean. Cool 5 minutes; remove from pans. Cool completely; frost as desired. *8 to 10 servings.*

*To Sour Milk: Use 1 tablespoon vinegar plus milk to equal 1 cup.
**Use ½ teaspoon vinegar plus milk to equal 3 tablespoons.

Chocolatetown Fudge Cake

¾ cup Hershey's Cocoa	1 teaspoon vanilla
½ cup sugar	1⅓ cups unsifted all-purpose
½ cup water	flour
¼ cup shortening	1 teaspoon baking soda
½ cup butter or margarine	1 teaspoon salt
1¼ cups sugar	⅔ cup milk
3 eggs	

Combine cocoa and ½ cup sugar in a saucepan; add water and shortening. Cook over low heat, stirring constantly, until shortening is melted and sugar is dissolved. Remove from heat; cool. Cream butter or margarine with 1¼ cups sugar in large mixer bowl. Add eggs, one at a time, beating after each addition. Add vanilla. Combine flour, baking soda and salt; add alternately with milk to creamed mixture. Blend in chocolate mixture. Pour into two greased and floured 9-inch layer pans. Bake at 350°F for 35 to 40 minutes or until cake tester inserted comes out clean. Cool 10 minutes; remove from pans. Cool completely; frost as desired. *8 to 10 servings.*

Classic Chocolate Cake

¾ cup Hershey's Cocoa	2 eggs
⅔ cup boiling water	2 cups unsifted cake flour
¾ cup butter or margarine,	1¼ teaspoons baking soda
softened	¼ teaspoon salt
2 cups sugar	¾ cup buttermilk or
1 teaspoon vanilla	sour milk*

Stir together cocoa and boiling water in small bowl until smooth; set aside. Cream butter or margarine, sugar and vanilla in large mixer bowl; blend in eggs. Combine flour, baking soda and salt; add alternately with buttermilk or sour milk to creamed mixture. Blend in reserved cocoa mixture. Pour batter into two greased and floured 9-inch layer pans. Bake at 350°F for 35 to 40 minutes or until cake tester inserted comes out clean. Cool 10 minutes; remove from pans. Cool completely; frost as desired.

*To Sour Milk: Use 2 teaspoons vinegar plus milk to equal ¾ cup.

How to Frost a Layer Cake

Brush loose crumbs from sides of unfrosted cake layers. Place first layer, top-side-down, on cake plate. Using a metal spatula or broad-bladed knife, spread frosting on the inverted layer. Place second layer, right-side-up, evenly on bottom layer. Then frost the sides of both layers, spreading frosting slightly over the top edge. Then frost the top. Blend the top frosting with the frosting on the sides.

Triple Spiced Crinoline Cake

¾ cup shortening
1¼ cups packed light brown
    sugar
1 cup sugar
2 eggs
1½ teaspoons vanilla
2⅔ cups unsifted cake flour
⅔ cup Hershey's Cocoa

1 teaspoon baking powder
¾ teaspoon salt
¾ teaspoon cinnamon
½ teaspoon baking soda
¼ teaspoon ginger
⅛ teaspoon nutmeg
1½ cups buttermilk or
    sour milk*

Cream shortening, brown sugar and sugar in mixer bowl. Add eggs and vanilla; blend well. Combine flour, cocoa, baking powder, salt, cinnamon, baking soda, ginger and nutmeg; add alternately with buttermilk or sour milk to creamed mixture, beating well after each addition. Pour into three greased and floured 8-inch round cake pans. Bake at 350°F for 30 to 40 minutes or until cake tester inserted comes out clean. Cool 10 minutes; remove from pans. Cool completely. Frost as desired. *10 to 12 servings.*

To Sour Milk: Use 1½ tablespoons vinegar plus milk to equal 1½ cups.

Hula-Hoop Marble Cheesecake

9-inch baked graham
    cracker crust
2 packages (8 ounces each)
    cream cheese, softened
1 cup sugar

2 tablespoons cornstarch
2 eggs, slightly beaten
1 teaspoon vanilla
¼ cup Hershey's Cocoa

Prepare crumb crust; cool. Beat cream cheese, ¾ cup sugar and cornstarch in large mixer bowl on medium speed until smooth. Beat in eggs and vanilla. Measure 1 cup batter; set aside. Combine cocoa and remaining ¼ cup sugar; beat cocoa mixture into remaining 2 cups batter in bowl until well blended. Pour chocolate and reserved vanilla batter alternately into crust. Gently swirl with spatula; bake at 350°F for 35 to 40 minutes or until center is firm. Cool completely on wire rack. Refrigerate 4 hours or overnight. *About 12 servings.*

Easy Fruit Toppings

Add ½ cup fruit preserves to 1½ cups fresh or canned fruit. Stir until fruit is coated, then arrange on top of any cheesecake.

Note: Sliced peaches, pineapple chunks, orange sections or fresh strawberries are especially good.

(Top to bottom) Triple Spiced Crinoline Cake with Classic Buttercream Cocoa Frosting, Hula-Hoop Marble Cheesecake

*t*he Sixties

*American prosperities, British pop music,
strides to equality, steps on the moon . . .
and chocolate frostings for all occasions*

When John F. Kennedy took office in 1961, he became America's youngest president and the first one born in the twentieth century. His inaugural speech carried the message: "The torch has been passed to a new generation."

The new generation was wealthier, more mobile and better educated than its predecessors. By 1960, the gross national product was more than twice that of 1945; it would rise another sixty percent by the end of the decade. Individual incomes grew by an average of eighty-five percent during the sixties; each year, a million new jobs were created. And between 1960 and 1970, the percentage of high school graduates jumped from sixty-five to seventy-nine percent of the population over 16. (Forty percent of those eligible were on college campuses by 1970.) The statistics added up to great freedom of choice, ranging from choice of profession and place of employment to choice of home, cars, furnishings and lifestyle.

The hopes of the decade were blinded by tears on November 22, 1963, when President Kennedy was assassinated. But President Lyndon Baines Johnson renewed the promises of the "New Frontier" and expanded them in his "Great Society" programs. In his 1964 State of the Union address, he declared "unconditional war on poverty." Under the president's direction, the Eighty-ninth Congress provided jobs for residents of urban ghettos and Appalachian hamlets, health insurance for the aged and indigent, and educational assistance for students enrolled in any kind of school. Concern for the quality of life brought legislative provisions for highway safety and beautification, improved housing and mass transit, plus efforts to clean up rivers and lakes. And all of this was accompanied by a tax cut. So whether people benefited from improved health care, new job skills, a college loan or some extra money left in their paychecks, they had reason to agree with Speaker of the House John W. McCormick, who called the Eighty-ninth "the Congress of realized dreams."

With the Civil Rights Act of 1965, which banned racial discrimination in public accommodations, and the Voting Rights Act of 1965, Congress addressed the dream summoned by Reverend Martin Luther King, Jr. Speaking to 200,000 civil rights supporters gathered in Washington, D.C., on August 28, 1963, Dr. King said, "Even though we face the difficulties of today and tomorrow, I still have a dream. It is a dream chiefly rooted in the American dream." It was a dream of justice and peace; it envisioned that "one day on the red hills of Georgia, the sons of former slaves and sons of former slave-owners will be able to sit together at the table of brotherhood."

Dr. King's dream came to symbolize the great strides toward equality achieved during the sixties, and his advocacy of nonviolence won him the

*The American flag
flies on the moon!
July, 1969*

The Beatles
(left to right)
Ringo Starr,
George Harrison,
John Lennon
and Paul McCartney

Nobel Peace Price in 1964. Fortunately, the dream didn't end when Dr. King was assassinated by a gunman in 1968. By the year of his death, there were 434,000 Afro-American students enrolled in colleges—in a nation where only half a decade earlier it had taken 30,000 federal troups to safeguard the right of one black Air Force veteran, James H. Meredith, to register for classes at the University of Mississippi.

Sounds of confrontations and protest were signs of the sixties—but they were not necessarily the loudest. That dubious honor could have been accorded the millions of screaming fans who welcomed a mop-headed English quartet to America in 1964. Crowds went wild when the Beatles sang a simple little ditty called "I Want to Hold Your Hand." And when the boys from Liverpool followed up with "She Loves You," everyone chorused, "yeah, yeah, yeah."

American artists also continued to secure top places on the pop charts, with the "Motown sound" exemplified by the Supremes and the Temptations, with lovely melodies written by such innovators as Simon and Garfunkel and with movie themes such as "Raindrops Keep Fallin' on My Head" from *Butch Cassidy and the Sundance Kid.*

President Kennedy had set an active pace for the decade with his call for physical fitness programs—and Chubby Checker answered with the agility standards of "the twist" and "limbo rock." A chef named Julia Child taught millions of TV viewers how to indulge in sauces and souffles—while the example set by a spindly, mini-skirted model called "Twiggy" drove many of those viewers to regret it! Biologist Rachel Carson warned that America must deal more wisely with its natural resources in her bestselling book, *Silent Spring—* while Snoopy and Charlie Brown championed the wisdom of beagles and moppets in the comic-strip world of "Peanuts." Andy Warhol created artworld controversy with his Pop Art paintings of soup cans; Tiny Tim betrayed musical harmonies with his off-key rendition of "Tiptoe Through the Tulips." And everyone found a new scapegoat for fouled-up billings and bank accounts in the early, creaky efforts of computers.

When the major technological feat of the times went off without a hitch, TV watchers saw the powdery surface of the moon broken by the footprints of astronauts Neil A. Armstrong and Edwin E. Aldrin, Jr. Some people couldn't believe their eyes; one woman told news reporters, "They're really not on the moon at all. They're just somewhere in New Jersey." Nevertheless, Armstrong and Aldrin marked their path with the message of the decade. It read: "Here men from the planet earth first set foot upon the moon, July 1969, A.D.: We came in peace for all mankind."

A Sixties Fondue Party

Select fondue recipe you prefer. Here are suggested fondue dippers for any of your favorite dessert fondues:

Fondue Dippers

Fruits	Other Treats
Strawberries	Marshmallows
Pineapple chunks	Ladyfingers
Grapes	Bite-size pieces of angel or pound cake
Cherries	Miniature cream puffs
Mandarin or fresh orange segments	Nuts
Apple slices*	Pretzels
Pear slices	Cookies
Peach slices	
Banana slices*	*Brush slices with lemon juice to prevent browning.

Let's Twist Again Fondue

1 cup Hershey's Chocolate Flavored Syrup
1 cup Hershey's Semi-Sweet Chocolate Mini Chips
¼ cup sweetened condensed milk

1 to 2 tablespoons brandy, ¼ teaspoon almond extract or 1 teaspoon vanilla
Fondue Dippers (see page 74)

Combine chocolate syrup, Mini Chips and condensed milk in heavy saucepan. Stir over low heat until thoroughly combined; add brandy, almond extract or vanilla. Pour into fondue pot or chafing dish; serve warm with selection of fondue dippers.
About 2 cups fondue.

Lift-Off Fluffy Vanilla Frosting

½ cup butter, margarine or shortening
5 cups confectioners' sugar

2 teaspoons vanilla
⅛ teaspoon salt
4 to 5 tablespoons milk

Cream butter, margarine or shortening, 1 cup confectioners' sugar, vanilla and salt in large mixer bowl. Add remaining confectioners' sugar alternately with milk, beating to spreading consistency.
About 3 cups frosting.

Let's Twist Again Fondue

Miniskirt Fondue

1 cup Hershey's Semi-Sweet
   Chocolate Chips or 2 cups
   Hershey's Milk Chocolate
   Chips
½ cup light cream

1 teaspoon vanilla or ⅛
   teaspoon almond extract
Fondue Dippers
   (see page 74)

Combine semi-sweet chocolate chips or milk chocolate chips and cream in heavy saucepan or place in top of double boiler over warm water. Stir until chips are melted and mixture is smooth; add vanilla or almond extract. Pour into fondue pot or chafing dish; serve warm with selection of fondue dippers. *About 1 cup semi-sweet or 1½ cups milk chocolate fondue.*

Mint Variation: Omit vanilla; add 1 tablespoon creme de menthe and 2 to 3 tablespoons creme de cacao.

Flower Power Fondue

2 Hershey's Milk Chocolate
   Bars (½ pound each)
4 ounces Hershey's
   Semi-Sweet Baking
   Chocolate
¾ cup light cream

2 to 3 tablespoons kirsch
   or orange-flavored liqueur
   or ½ teaspoon almond
   extract (optional)
Fondue Dippers
   (see page 74)

Combine chocolate bars, baking chocolate and cream in a heavy saucepan; stir constantly over medium-low heat until chocolate is melted. Just before serving, add liqueur or almond extract, if desired; pour into fondue pot or chafing dish. Serve warm with a selection of fondue dippers. *About 2½ cups fondue.*

Seven Minute Frosting

2 egg whites
1½ cups sugar

⅓ cup water
1½ teaspoons vanilla

Combine egg whites, sugar and water in top of double boiler over boiling water; beat about 7 minutes at high speed or until frosting holds its shape. Remove from heat; beat in vanilla.
About 3 cups frosting.

Cocoa Seven Minute Frosting: Carefully fold in ¼ cup Hershey's Cocoa with vanilla.

Chocolate Glaze

2 tablespoons butter or
  margarine
2 tablespoons Hershey's
  Cocoa

2 tablespoons water
1 cup confectioners' sugar
½ teaspoon vanilla

Melt butter or margarine in small saucepan over low heat; add cocoa
and water, stirring constantly, until mixture thickens. Do not boil.
Remove from heat; blend in confectioners' sugar and vanilla.
About ½ cup glaze.

Very-Best-Ever Hot Fudge Sauce!

½ cup heavy cream
¼ cup butter or
  margarine, cut into
  pieces
½ cup sugar

½ cup packed light brown
  sugar
Pinch of salt
½ cup Hershey's Cocoa
1 teaspoon vanilla

Heat cream and butter or margarine in medium saucepan until butter
or margarine is melted and cream is beginning to boil; stir in sugars
and salt. Cook over medium heat, stirring constantly, until sugars
are dissolved, about 3 minutes. Remove from heat; stir or whisk in
cocoa and vanilla until blended. Serve immediately or cool to room
temperature, cover, and refrigerate. *About 1¼ cups sauce.*

Note: If sugar crystals form after refrigerating, add 1 tablespoon hot
water to sauce when heating. Heat to boiling, stirring constantly,
until smooth.

New Frontier Caramel Frosting

⅓ cup butter or margarine
1 cup packed light brown
  sugar
⅓ cup light cream or
  evaporated milk

2 ounces Hershey's
  Semi-Sweet Baking
  Chocolate
2 cups confectioners' sugar
1 teaspoon vanilla

Melt butter or margarine in small saucepan; add brown sugar and
light cream or evaporated milk. Bring to boil over low heat, stirring
constantly; boil and stir 1 minute. Remove from heat; add semi-
sweet chocolate stirring until blended. Pour into mixer bowl; cool
without stirring to room temperature. Add confectioners' sugar and
vanilla; beat to spreading consistency. Additional light cream or
evaporated milk may be needed. *About 2 cups frosting.*

Classic Buttercream Cocoa Frosting

3½ cups confectioners' sugar
⅔ cup Hershey's Cocoa
⅓ cup butter or margarine

½ cup milk or evaporated milk
1 teaspoon vanilla

Combine confectioners' sugar and cocoa in bowl. Cream butter or margarine and ½ cup of cocoa mixture in large mixer bowl until well blended. Gradually add milk or evaporated milk and vanilla. Blend in remaining cocoa mixture, beating to spreading consistency. *About 2 cups frosting.*

Memory-Making Fudge Frosting

½ cup butter or margarine
½ cup Hershey's Cocoa
3⅔ cups (1-pound box) confectioners' sugar

5 to 6 tablespoons milk
1 teaspoon vanilla

Melt butter or margarine over low heat in small saucepan; add cocoa. Cook, stirring constantly, just until mixture begins to boil. Remove from heat; pour into small mixer bowl. Add confectioners' sugar alternately with milk. Beat to spreading consistency; blend in vanilla. Spread frosting while warm. *About 2 cups frosting.*

Mint Variation: Add 1 tablespoon finely crushed peppermint candy.

Whipped Cream Filling

1 cup heavy cream
½ cup confectioners' sugar

2 tablespoons Hershey's Cocoa
½ teaspoon vanilla

Whip cream until slightly thickened. Add confectioners' sugar, cocoa and vanilla; whip until stiff. *About 2 cups cream filling.*

Creamy Mocha Frosting

2⅔ cups confectioners' sugar
¼ cup Hershey's Cocoa
6 tablespoons butter or shortening

1 teaspoon instant coffee granules
3 to 4 tablespoons milk
1 teaspoon vanilla

Combine confectioners' sugar and cocoa in bowl. Cream butter or shortening with ½ cup cocoa mixture in small bowl. Dissolve coffee granules in milk; add alternately with remaining cocoa mixture, beating to spreading consistency. Blend in vanilla.
About 2 cups frosting.

California Dream Chocolate Sauce

1 box (4-ounce bar) Hershey's Sweet Baking Chocolate	1 tablespoon honey or light corn syrup
¼ cup sweet butter	2 tablespoons heavy cream
	½ teaspoon vanilla

Melt chocolate with butter and honey or corn syrup in small saucepan over very low heat, stirring constantly. Blend in cream and vanilla; serve warm over ice cream or desserts. Refrigerate any remaining sauce. *About ¾ cup sauce.*

Classic Chocolate Sauce

2 ounces Hershey's Unsweetened Baking Chocolate	1 cup sugar
	¼ teaspoon salt
	¾ cup evaporated milk
2 tablespoons butter or margarine	½ teaspoon vanilla

Melt baking chocolate and butter or margarine in saucepan over low heat, stirring occasionally. Stir in sugar and salt; add evaporated milk and blend well. Cook, stirring constantly, until mixture just begins to boil. Remove from heat; add vanilla. Serve warm over ice cream or other dessert. *About 2 cups sauce.*

Moon Walk Peanut Butter Sauce

½ cup Reese's Peanut Butter Chips	3 tablespoons evaporated milk
⅓ cup Hershey's Chocolate Flavored Syrup	1 tablespoon butter

Combine all ingredients in small saucepan. Stir constantly over low heat until mixture is smooth. Serve warm over ice cream or other dessert. *About 1 cup sauce.*

Quick Chocolate Frosting

2 ounces Hershey's Unsweetened Baking Chocolate	1½ cups confectioners' sugar
	½ teaspoon vanilla
	Dash salt
2 tablespoons butter or margarine	3 to 4 tablespoons evaporated milk

Melt baking chocolate and butter or margarine in small saucepan over low heat, stirring constantly, until smooth. Pour into small mixer bowl; add confectioners' sugar, vanilla and salt. Blend in evaporated milk; beat to spreading consistency (additional evaporated milk may be needed). *About 1 cup frosting.*

the Seventies

celebrating 200 hundred years of American progress with parades, jogathons, star ships . . . and freshly baked breads

If America's Founding Fathers could have returned for our Bicentennial, they would have heard the Liberty Bell tolling in Philadelphia and would have seen the Battle of Bunker Hill re-enacted in Massachusetts. In New York City, they would have been greeted by an armada of square-rigged ships and sailboats. And in the town of George, Washington, they could have feasted on a 60-square-foot cherry pie.

But if Washington, Adams and Jefferson had decided simply to take a stroll down America's streets, they would have risked being trampled by a horde of joggers and sideswiped by a flotilla of skateboard champs! They could have been dizzied by the blinking lights of thousands of discos and dazzled by movie marquees bearing the odd title, *Jaws*. And if they had stopped to ask directions of a woman sporting blue jeans embroidered with somebody's name or a man attired in a "Save the Seals" T-shirt, they no doubt would have been cheered by the parting words, "Have a nice day!"

If the historic leaders could have caught up with the decade's headlines, they might have been pleased to learn how well the United States Constitution had weathered the scandals of President Richard Nixon's administration. The successive resignations of the vice-president and the president had not resulted in chaos. Instead, leadership had passed in an orderly manner to President Gerald Ford, the first man whose worthiness of the office had not been tested by popular vote. Freedom of speech and of the press had guaranteed that the burglary and bungling of Watergate would become grist for the mills of best-selling books and confessional talk shows. Nor would evidence of President Nixon's prouder moments be erased: two playful giant pandas, Hsing-Hsing and Ling-Ling, would remind Washingtonians of the president's 1972 peace-making walk along the Great Wall of China; continued strategic arms limitation talks would reinforce the achievement of detente with the Soviet Union; and the promise of an end to the war in Vietnam would be fulfilled in 1975.

The Founding Fathers would have discovered that Americans of the seventies looked both forward and back. The futuristic fantasy of *Star*

Boats and ships jam New York harbor, July 4, 1976, to celebrate America's Bicentennial

Jogging, evidence of the nation's new health awareness in the seventies

Wars earned a record-breaking $400 million at movie box offices. But the largest television audience—130 million people—tuned in for the historic saga of Alex Haley's *Roots*. And millions of people turned back the clock to enjoy the 1920's fashions revived by the movie, *The Great Gatsby*. The 1930's comic-strip charms of Little Orphan Annie drew crowds to Broadway's hit musical, *Annie*. The crazy-mixed-up fun of 1950's teenagers, as depicted in the theater and movie versions of *Grease*, inspired both nostalgia and widespread imitation. Yet people gladly traded old-fashioned pencil and paper for the convenience of new-fashioned pocket calculators. Many benefited from medical advances in X-ray diagnostic techniques and coronary bypass surgery. And newswatchers everywhere were awed by the landing of Viking robots on Mars.

If confusion characterized the seventies, there were reasons for it. Unemployment reached the highest rate since the Great Depression of the thirties, and inflation soared to the level recorded just after World War I. The terrorist attack on the Munich Olympics of 1972 and the nuclear power accident at Three Mile Island in 1979 compounded national fears. Yet the nation's disposable income rose by 28.5 percent; so anxious consumers could find distraction in such novelties as hot tubs, snowmobiles, video tape recorders, mopeds and CB radios. And the prospects of peace looked better than ever when President Jimmy Carter brought Middle East leaders Anwar Sadat and Menachim Begin to the point of accord at Camp David.

It was only natural that amidst all the contradictions a hero should emerge whom nobody liked but everybody loved. Every week on television, *All in the Family's* Archie Bunker set things straight—only to be set straight himself by the "dingbat" and "meathead" who shared his home. A belligerent Archie confronted the issue of women's rights head-on by telling his wife, "All right, Edith, you go right ahead and do your thing. . .but just remember that your thing is eggs over-easy and crisp bacon!" Television audiences sat back and laughed, for they knew that all the while Archie was hollering, women—for the first time—were "doing their thing" as telephone linepersons, airline pilots, Rhodes scholars, astronauts, Episcopalian ministers and midshipmen at the United States Naval Academy.

AMERICAN REVOLUTION BICENTENNIAL 1776-1976

The Bicentennial Emblem

King Tut Golden Muffins

¼ cup butter or margarine, melted	⅓ cup sugar
½ cup sour cream	¼ cup Hershey's Cocoa
⅔ cup (8-ounce can) crushed pineapple, drained	1 teaspoon baking powder
	¼ teaspoon baking soda
1 egg, slightly beaten	¼ teaspoon salt
1 cup unsifted all-purpose flour	¼ cup chopped nuts
	Pop Art Sugar Glaze (optional) (page 87)

Thoroughly blend melted butter or margarine, sour cream, drained pineapple and egg in small bowl. Combine flour, sugar, cocoa, baking powder, baking soda, salt and nuts; blend well. Add pineapple mixture to dry ingredients; stir just until moistened. Fill well-greased or paper-lined muffin cups (2½ inches in diameter) ¾ full; bake at 400°F for 20 minutes or until cake tester inserted comes out clean. Remove from pan; cool on wire rack. Glaze, if desired. *12 muffins.*

Loaf Variation: Spoon batter into a greased and floured 8½ X 4½-inch loaf pan; bake at 350°F for 55 to 60 minutes or until cake tester inserted comes out clean. Cool 10 minutes; remove from pan. *One loaf.*

Disco Berry Loaf

2 cups unsifted all-purpose flour	2 tablespoons shortening
1 cup sugar	1 egg, slightly beaten
1½ teaspoons baking powder	1 cup chopped fresh cranberries
1 teaspoon salt	1 cup Hershey's Semi-Sweet Chocolate Mini Chips
½ teaspoon baking soda	
¾ cup orange juice	¾ cup chopped nuts
1 teaspoon grated orange peel	Glaze (optional) (recipe below)

Combine flour, sugar, baking powder, salt and baking soda in large mixing bowl. Add orange juice, orange peel, shortening and egg; mix with spoon until well blended. Stir in cranberries, Mini Chips and nuts. Pour into greased 9 X 5 X 3-inch loaf pan. Bake at 350°F for 65 to 70 minutes or until toothpick inserted comes out clean. Cool 10 minutes; remove from pan. Glaze, if desired, or garnish with cranberries and lemon leaves. *1 loaf.*

Glaze: Combine 1 cup confectioners' sugar, 1 teaspoon butter or margarine, 1 tablespoon milk and ½ teaspoon vanilla. (If thinner glaze is desired, add additional milk, a teaspoonful at a time.)

(Top to bottom) Joggers Harvest Ring, King Tut Golden Muffins, Nostalgia Date-Nut Loaves; Disco Berry Loaf

Joggers Harvest Ring

¾ cup unsifted whole wheat flour*	¾ cup vegetable oil
¾ cup unsifted all-purpose flour	1½ teaspoons vanilla
¾ cup sugar	2 cups grated carrot, apple or zucchini, drained
½ cup packed brown sugar	¾ cup Hershey's Semi-Sweet Chocolate Mini Chips
2 teaspoons cinnamon	½ cup chopped walnuts
1¼ teaspoons baking soda	Cream Cheese Glaze
½ teaspoon salt	(recipe below)
3 eggs	

Combine flours, sugar, brown sugar, cinnamon, baking soda and salt in large bowl. Beat eggs, oil and vanilla in small bowl; add to dry ingredients and blend. Stir in carrot, apple or zucchini, Mini Chips and walnuts. Pour into greased and floured 6-cup or 8-cup Bundt pan. Bake at 350°F for 45 to 50 minutes or until cake tester inserted comes out clean. Cool 30 minutes; remove from pan. Spread with Cream Cheese Glaze. *8 to 10 servings.*

All-purpose flour may be substituted for whole wheat flour.

Cream Cheese Glaze: Beat 3 ounces cream cheese until smooth in small bowl; blend in 1½ cups confectioners' sugar, 1 tablespoon milk and 1 teaspoon vanilla. Beat until spreading consistency. Spoon over bread.

Nostalgia Date-Nut Loaves

1½ cups boiling water	2 teaspoons baking soda
1 cup pitted dates, chopped	½ teaspoon salt
1¼ cups sugar	¼ teaspoon baking powder
1 egg	1 cup chopped nuts
1 tablespoon vegetable oil	1 cup Hershey's Semi-Sweet Chocolate Mini Chips
2 teaspoons vanilla	Walnut halves (optional)
2 cups unsifted all-purpose flour	

Pour boiling water over dates; let stand 15 minutes. Beat sugar and egg 3 minutes on high speed. Blend in oil and vanilla. Combine flour, baking soda, salt and baking powder; add alternately with dates to egg mixture. Blend well. Stir in nuts and Mini Chips. Pour one generous cup of batter into each of four well-greased mini loaf pans (3¼ × 5¾ × 2¼ inches) or into four 16-ounce cans (about 3 inches in diameter). Bake at 350°F for 40 to 50 minutes or until cake tester inserted comes out clean. Cool 10 minutes; remove from pans. Garnish with walnut halves if desired.

4 loaves.

"Have a Nice Day" Walnut Kuchen with two-tone Pop Art Sugar Glaze, Bicentennial Peach Coffeecake

"Have a Nice Day" Walnut Kuchen

2½ to 2¾ cups unsifted
  all-purpose flour
¼ cup sugar
½ teaspoon salt
 1 package active dry yeast
½ cup sour cream
¼ cup water
 2 tablespoons milk

¼ cup butter or margarine
 2 egg yolks, room
  temperature (reserve
  whites for filling)
"Mod" Nut-Chip Filling
  (recipe below)
Pop Art Sugar Glaze
  (optional) (page 87)

Mix 1 cup flour, sugar, salt and undissolved active dry yeast in a large mixer bowl; set aside. Combine sour cream, water, milk and butter or margarine in small saucepan. Place over low heat until liquids are very warm (120°F to 130°F). Gradually add to dry ingredients; beat 2 minutes at medium speed. Add egg yolks and ½ cup flour; beat 2 minutes at high speed. Gradually stir in enough flour to make a soft dough. When dough becomes difficult to stir, turn out onto well-floured board. Knead in enough remaining flour until dough is elastic and forms a smooth ball (about 3 to 5 minutes). Cover; allow to rest 15 minutes. Divide dough into 2 equal pieces.

On a lightly floured board, roll out each piece of dough to a 12 × 10-inch rectangle. Spread 1 cup of "Mod" Nut-Chip Filling to within ½ inch of edges. Roll up dough from long side as for jelly roll; pinch to seal edges. For roll, crescent or spiral, place on greased cookie sheet, sealed edges down, curving rolls to form desired shape. To prepare roll with seam on top, fill and roll as described above and place on greased cookie sheet, sealed edge up, just slightly curving roll. Cover with plastic wrap or towel and let rise in a warm place until doubled in bulk, about 1 to 1½ hours.

Bake at 350°F for 20 minutes. Loosely cover with aluminum foil and bake 15 minutes longer or until golden brown. Remove from oven and brush lightly with butter or margarine. Cool completely on wire rack. Just before serving, sprinkle with confectioners' sugar or glaze with Pop Art Sugar Glaze. Garnish as desired. 2 loaves.

"Mod" Nut-Chip Filling

2 egg whites, room
  temperature
⅓ cup sugar
 Dash salt

2 cups ground walnuts
1 cup Hershey's Semi-Sweet
  Chocolate Mini Chips

Beat egg whites until foamy in small mixer bowl. Gradually add sugar and salt beating until stiff peaks form. Fold in ground walnuts and Mini Chips; blend well. About 2 cups filling.

Pop Art Sugar Glaze

¾ cup confectioners' sugar   ½ to 1 tablespoon milk
¼ teaspoon vanilla

Blend confectioners' sugar, vanilla and milk until smooth.

Two-Tone Glaze: Pour half of glaze into small bowl; stir in 1 tablespoon cocoa. Drizzle with vanilla and cocoa glazes as desired.

Bicentennial Peach Coffeecake

⅓ cup apricot or peach
   preserves
2 cups sliced peaches
1 tablespoon lemon juice
   Maraschino or dark,
   sweet cherries
1½ cups unsifted all-purpose
   flour
½ cup sugar

1½ teaspoons baking powder
½ teaspoon salt
½ teaspoon cinnamon
½ cup butter or margarine
1 egg, slightly beaten
½ cup milk
½ teaspoon vanilla
½ cup Hershey's Semi-Sweet
   Chocolate Mini Chips

Line an 8 × 2-inch round layer pan with wax paper. Spread apricot or peach preserves evenly in bottom. Toss peach slices with lemon juice; arrange with cherries in decorative design.

Combine flour, sugar, baking powder, salt and cinnamon in large mixing bowl. Cut in butter or margarine until mixture resembles fine crumbs. Combine egg, milk and vanilla; add to dry ingredients, stirring until blended (batter appears slightly lumpy). Stir in Mini Chips; spread batter carefully over fruit. Bake at 350°F for 45 to 50 minutes or until cake tester inserted comes out clean. Immediately invert onto serving plate; carefully remove wax paper. Serve warm.

8 to 10 servings.

Do You Bake with Oven-proof Glassware?

Most recipes for baked goods—including those in this book—call for oven temperatures suitable for baking with metal pans. If you use oven-proof glassware, reduce the oven temperature by 25 degrees to prevent over-baking.

the Eighties

*welcoming the age of the Space Shuttle
with predictions, prophesies . . .
and the speed of microwave sweets*

Scientists base their predictions for the eighties on the achievements of previous decades. And the prospects are astonishing.

Just as automobiles pushed aside horse-drawn vehicles in the twenties, and television entered most households during the fifties, so computers may become commonplace in the eighties. When the technology now available acquires a popular price tag, people will be able to check their home computers for the latest health information, weather reports, news headlines and supermarket specials. Bridge and chess players will be able to set a game time with any other computer-owner in the world. Adult education will take on the added allure of individualized instruction in foreign languages, finance and philosophy—while children's homework will be transformed by electronic teachers' "dirty looks!"

Youngsters will be advised to study not only science, medicine and engineering but also cooking, cosmetology and retail etiquette. Government statistics indicate that tomorrow's employment will be found both in industries that maximize the benefits of technology and in services that promote the pleasures of leisure. Agricul-ture will account for only two percent of all job openings, and blue collar work for less than one-fourth.

Some people will be doing a lot of traveling, and their luggage could be tagged "Moon," "Mars" and "Space Station Observatory." It is conceivable that miners will be sent to the moon to replenish the earth's stock of minerals. And astronomers might book passage on the Space Shuttle to survey the universe through a telescope set up amidst the stars. Electrical engineers could be monitoring photovoltaic cells stretched across the Sahara, as the possibility of harnessing solar energy efficiently and economically becomes a reality. Ecologists may see trash heaps recycled by a special process of heating and cooling that will quickly break down discarded materials and restore them to useful components. But biologists may have to retreat to easy chairs to study new laws of scientific ethics, because the age of cloning has arrived.

*Left, the Space Shuttle;
above, a telephone
console and word
processor*

Justice Sandra Day O'Connor, the first woman named to the Supreme Court, is sworn in, August 15, 1981

If Milton Hershey were to appraise these many developments, he might be less surprised than the rest of us. After all, as a boy of five-going-on-six, he heard news of the Battle of Gettysburg, fought just 50 miles from his home. As a middle-aged man, he drove the first car ever seen in Lancaster, Pennsylvania—a Riker Electric that could overtake cows and pedestrians at its top speed of nine miles per hour. And not long before he died in 1945, he learned that America had entered the nuclear age.

What might startle (and please) the chocolate-maker would be a tally of things that remain unchanged in the eighties—especially in the town of Hershey. The pace set by Hershey's Riker Electric of 1900 is celebrated annually by the thousands of antique-car buffs who flock to events scheduled by the National Headquarters of the Antique Automobile Club of America, which was established in Hershey in 1959. Visitors and local residents still relax in the rose garden planted by Catherine Hershey, which now flourishes amidst 23 acres planted with 120,000 types of flowers, trees and shrubs.

The Hershey tradition of hospitality also continues at Chocolate World, where a simulation of the chocolate-making process was created in 1973 to accommodate the ever-growing number of visitors who had enjoyed Hershey plant tours since early in the century. Chocolate World now welcomes 1.6 million people annually. It is free and open year-round.

Milton Hershey would be touched by the sight of the little desks and oil lamps that have been restored to Derry Church School, the one-room alma mater of his youth. He would be especially gratified to see that the Milton Hershey School (renamed from the "Hershey Industrial School" in 1951) now has an enrollment of 1400 boys *and* girls, as well as facilities for students to learn skills unheard of when Hershey was a child. And he would be proud that funds from his trust went to endow the Milton S. Hershey Medical Center of Pennsylvania State University, which has trained hundreds of physicians since its dedication in 1971.

"What I want to do is to find a practical use for what I have," Milton Hershey once said, "and to put it to work in a way that will benefit others." His wish became a prediction that is still being fulfilled—even as his chocolate continues to create memories for the pioneers of tomorrow.

For more information about Chocolate Town, U.S.A., write to:
Hershey's Chocolate World
Department C, Park Boulevard
Hershey, PA 17033

New-Fashioned Chocolate Mousse

1 envelope unflavored
  gelatine
¾ cup milk
½ cup sugar
⅛ teaspoon salt
3 egg yolks, slightly
  beaten
1 cup Hershey's
  Semi-Sweet Chocolate
  Mini Chips

¼ cup milk
1 teaspoon vanilla
3 egg whites
2 tablespoons sugar
½ cup heavy cream
Additional sweetened
  whipped cream
  (optional)
Strawberries (optional)

Soften gelatine in ¾ cup milk a few minutes in small glass bowl; microwave on high (full power) about 1½ minutes, or until gelatine is dissolved. Blend in ½ cup sugar, salt and egg yolks; set aside. Combine Mini Chips and ¼ cup milk in glass mixing bowl. Microwave on high 1½ minutes; stir until melted. Gradually add gelatine mixture to melted chocolate. Microwave on high 2 to 2½ minutes, stirring after 1½ minutes, or until mixture is very hot; do not boil. Stir in vanilla. Press plastic wrap onto surface of chocolate mixture; chill until mixture mounds from spoon. Beat egg whites in small mixer bowl until foamy; beat in 2 tablespoons sugar until stiff. Whip cream until stiff. Fold stiffly beaten egg whites and cream into chocolate mixture. Spoon mixture into individual dessert dishes or serving bowl. Chill until set; garnish with additional whipped cream or strawberries, if desired. *6 to 8 servings.*

Chocolate Mousse Pie: Spoon mixture into 9-inch graham cracker or baked pastry shell. Chill thoroughly. Garnish as above.

Kiss-Me-Quick Teacakes

1 cup butter or margarine
½ cup confectioners' sugar
1 egg
1 teaspoon vanilla
2⅓ cups unsifted all-purpose
  flour

½ cup finely chopped nuts
9-ounce package
  (about 54) Hershey's
  Milk Chocolate Kisses,
  unwrapped
Confectioners' sugar

Beat softened butter or margarine, confectioners' sugar, egg and vanilla until light and fluffy. Blend in flour and nuts. Shape about 1 tablespoon dough around each chocolate kiss, covering completely. Place 12 cookies on paper towel-covered microwave baking sheet. Microwave on high (full power) for about 2 minutes, turning ¼ turn every 30 seconds, or until surface appears dry. Cool on baking sheet for 5 minutes; remove and cool. Roll in confectioners' sugar. Store in covered container; roll again in confectioners' sugar before serving. *About 4 dozen cookies.*

New-Fashioned Chocolate Mousse

Important Microwave Hints

Most microwave ovens today range between 600 and 700 watts, so the high setting is fairly standard. Lower levels of power are not standard, however, as they vary from one brand and model of microwave oven to another. Lower powers in these recipes are listed according to percentage of power.

High	equals	full power	or	600 to 700 watts
Medium-high	equals	2/3 power	or	425 to 475 watts
Medium	equals	1/2 power	or	300 to 350 watts
Low	equals	1/3 power	or	175 to 225 watts
Warm	equals			75 to 125 watts

Keep in mind that cooking times given in the recipes are *guidelines* that will vary according to the cooking pattern and wattage of your particular microwave oven. For this reason, rely on the desired result (i.e., microwave for 5 minutes, or "until mixture boils") to determine "doneness."

Results are more consistent if food is stirred or rotated several times during microwave cooking. Also, where cookies and muffins are involved, the cooking time is geared to the number of items called for in the recipe. If you are cooking fewer items, decrease the time; for more items, increase the time.

Easy Mocha Freeze

⅓ cup milk
2 teaspoons instant coffee
  granules
1 cup miniature
  marshmallows
½ cup Hershey's
  Semi-Sweet Chocolate
  Chips

¼ cup chopped almonds
1 tablespoon brandy
  (optional)
1 teaspoon vanilla
1½ cups non-dairy whipped
  topping

Mix milk and coffee granules in glass mixing bowl; add marshmallows and chocolate chips. Microwave on high (full power) just until boiling, about 1½ to 2 minutes; stir until smooth. Stir in almonds, brandy (if desired) and vanilla; cool. Fold whipped topping gently into chocolate mixture. Spoon into 8 paper-lined muffin cups, cover; freeze until firm. Serve with additional whipped topping, if desired. *8 servings.*

Time-Saver Streusel Cake

Streusel (recipe below)
½ cup butter or margarine
1 cup sugar
3 eggs
1 cup sour cream
1 teaspoon vanilla
2 cups unsifted all-purpose
  flour

1 teaspoon baking powder
1 teaspoon baking soda
¼ cup Hershey's
  Semi-Sweet Chocolate
  Mini Chips

Prepare Streusel; set aside. Cream butter or margarine and sugar in a large mixer bowl. Add eggs; blend on low speed. Stir in sour cream and vanilla. Combine flour, baking powder and baking soda; add to batter. Blend well. Sprinkle reserved 1 cup nut streusel mixture into greased 10 or 12-cup microwave Bundt cake or tube pan. Spread ⅓ of batter (about 1½ cups) in pan; sprinkle with ½ (about 1 cup) Mini Chip streusel. Repeat layers; end with batter on top. Loosely cover pan with wax paper. Place on microwave rack or inverted saucer; microwave on high (full power) for 10 to 12 minutes, rotating ¼ turn every 3 minutes, or until top appears dry and cake tester inserted comes out clean. Let stand 10 minutes. Loosen cake from sides and center of pan; invert onto serving plate. Sprinkle ¼ cup Mini Chips onto top; serve warm or cold. *10 to 12 servings.*

Streusel

¾ cup packed brown sugar
¼ cup butter or margarine
¼ cup unsifted all-purpose
  flour
¼ teaspoon salt

¼ teaspoon cinnamon
1 cup chopped walnuts
¾ cup Hershey's Semi-Sweet
  Chocolate Mini Chips

Combine brown sugar, butter or margarine, flour, salt and cinnamon in a small mixing bowl; stir until crumbly. Stir in nuts. Reserve one cup of nut streusel for bottom. Stir Mini Chips into remaining nut streusel.

Space Age Mallow Glaze

⅓ cup sugar
3 tablespoons water
1 cup Hershey's Semi-Sweet
  Chocolate Mini Chips

3 tablespoons marshmallow
  creme
Hot water

Combine sugar and 3 tablespoons water in small glass mixing bowl; microwave on high (full power) about 1 minute, or until boiling. Immediately add Mini Chips; stir until melted. Blend in marshmallow creme; add hot water, a teaspoonful at a time, until glaze is desired consistency. *About 1 cup glaze.*

Microwave Cookie Favorites

1 cup butter or margarine	⅔ cup Hershey's Cocoa
1½ cups sugar	¾ teaspoon baking soda
2 eggs	½ teaspoon salt
2 teaspoons vanilla	2 cups (12-ounce package)
2 cups unsifted all-purpose	Reese's Peanut Butter
flour	Chips

Cream butter or margarine, sugar, eggs and vanilla until light and fluffy. Combine flour, cocoa, baking soda and salt; add to creamed mixture. Stir in peanut butter chips. Chill until firm enough to handle; shape into 1-inch balls. Place 10 cookies on paper towel-covered microwave baking tray in circular formation; flatten slightly with fork. Microwave for 3½ to 4½ minutes on medium (½ power) turning ¼ turn every minute, or until set. *About 5 dozen cookies.*

Breakfast Bonus Muffins

1 cup unsifted all-purpose	½ cup milk
flour	¼ cup vegetable oil
⅔ cup sugar	1 egg, slightly beaten
¼ cup Hershey's Cocoa	1 cup raisins
2 teaspoons baking powder	½ cup chopped nuts
½ teaspoon salt	

Combine flour, sugar, cocoa, baking powder and salt in glass mixing bowl. Add milk, oil and egg all at once to dry ingredients; stir just until moistened. Fold in raisins and nuts. Fill 7 paper muffin cups ½ full; place in microwave cupcake or muffin maker. Microwave on high (full power) for about 2 to 2½ minutes, turning ¼ turn at 1 minute, 1½ minutes, and 2 minutes. Repeat cooking procedure with remaining batter. Serve warm; spread with butter or cream cheese, if desired. *14 muffins.*

Note: The cooking time for this recipe is geared to 7 muffins. If you are making less at one time, cooking time should be shortened.

Baking Terms

Beat: To combine and make smooth by rapid, vigorous motion using an electric mixer, rotary beater, wire whisk or spoon.

Blend: To thoroughly mix two or more ingredients.

Combine: To stir together two or more ingredients (usually dry) in a bowl.

Cream: To make smooth, light and fluffy by beating with a spoon or electric mixer.

Gradually add: To add liquid or dry ingredients in small amounts, for ease in blending and to prevent lumping.

Double-Fun Pie

9-inch Graham-Nut
Crust (recipe below)
1 package (8 one-ounce
blocks) Hershey's
Semi-Sweet Baking
Chocolate

⅓ cup milk
1½ cups miniature
marshmallows
1 cup heavy cream
1 cup miniature
marshmallows

Prepare crust; set aside. Break chocolate into pieces; place in glass mixing bowl. Add milk and 1½ cups miniature marshmallows. Microwave on high (full power) 1½ to 2 minutes or until hot. Remove from oven; stir occasionally until marshmallows and chocolate are melted. Cool. Whip cream until stiff; fold cream and 1 cup marshmallows into chocolate mixture. Spoon into pie crust; chill thoroughly. Garnish with additional marshmallows, if desired. *8 servings.*

Graham-Nut Crust

¼ cup butter or margarine
¾ cup finely chopped nuts

¾ cup graham cracker
crumbs
2 tablespoons sugar

Melt butter in 9-inch glass pie plate on high (full power) 35 to 45 seconds; stir in nuts, crumbs and sugar. Press crumbs firmly against bottom and up sides of pie plate. Microwave on high 1 to 1½ minutes or until golden brown. Cool.

More Storage Hints for Chocolate Products

Chocolate contains cocoa butter. Temperatures about 78°F cause chocolate to melt and cocoa butter to rise to the surface forming a gray discoloration known as "cocoa butter bloom." "Sugar bloom" may occur when condensation forms on the surface of semi-sweet or milk chocolate, causing sugar to dissolve and to rise to the surface. In both cases, the quality and flavor of the chocolate is not affected. Upon melting, the chocolate regains its original color.

Chocolate products generally stay fresh well over a year when stored correctly. To avoid "bloom," store chocolate in a cool, dry place where the temperature is about 70°F. Chocolate can be refrigerated during hot, humid weather, but in some instances, it may bloom when brought to room temperature.

Hershey's Baking Chocolate should be stored at room temperature. (It can be refrigerated during hot weather, because it contains no sugar and will not develop "sugar bloom.")

Other hints are found on page 36.

Recipe Index

Turn to pages set in *italic* type for colorful photographs that will guide you as you initiate some *Hershey Chocolate Memories* in your own home!

Beverages
Charleston Hot Chocolate, 36, *35*
Family Fun Cocoa, 37
Flapper's Slimmer, The, 37
Hershey's Chocoberry Splash, 34, *35*
Instant Shimmy Shake, 34, *35*
Jazz Age Eggnog, 37
Lucky Lindy Floats, 36
Old Fashioned Chocolate Soda, 34

Breads
Bicentennial Peach Coffeecake, 87, *85*
Disco Berry Loaf, 82, *83*
"Have a Nice Day" Walnut Kuchen, 86, *85*
Joggers Harvest Ring, 84, *83*
King Tut Golden Muffins, 82, *83*
Nostalgia Date-Nut Loaves, 84, *83*

Cakes
April Love Pecan Cake, 68
Bridge Party Coffee Cake, 68
Chantilly Lace Chiffon Cake, 62
Chocolatetown Fudge Cake, 69
Classic Chocolate Cake, 69
Drive-In Snack Cake, 65
Fan Club Fudge Cake, 63
Flying Saucer Crater Cake, 64
Hula-Hoop Marble Cheesecake, 70, *71*
Pedal Pushers Upside-Down Cake, 66, *67*
Pink Flamingo Cake Roll, 60, *61*
Pony Tail Pound Cake, 64
Sing-Along Swirl Cake, 63
3-D Cheesecake, 65
Triple Spiced Crinoline Cake, 70, *71*
Two-Tone Cup Cakes, 66

Candies
Chocolate Centers, 15
Chocolate Coatings, 16, 26
Chocolate-Dipped Cherry Cordials, 14, *13*
Chocolate Kiss Divinity, 12, *13*
Columbian Semi-Sweet Coating, 9
Double Decker Fudge, 12, *13*
Easy Semi-Sweet Coating, 10
Ferris Wheel Fudge, 11
Gay 90's Pulled Taffy, 6, *7*
Gibson Girl Bonbons, 6
Gilded-Age Truffles, 15, *13*
High Point Fudge Supreme, 11
Ragtime Rocky Road, 6
Trolley Car Nougat Chews, 16, *17*
Vaudeville Nugget Clusters, 10
Walnut Grove Toffee, 14, *13*

Cookies
Brown-Eyed Susans, 31
Bunny Hug Brownies, 27
Celebration Fudgey Brownies, 31
Chewy Homestead Brownies, 28, *29*
Chocolate Cream Cheese Brownies, 23
Chocolate Thumbprint Cookies, 27, *25*
Cocoa Kiss Cookies, 23
Double Chocolate Hits, 22
Hershey's Chocolate Chip Cookies, 20, *21*
Lickety-Split Cookies, 22
Mini Chip Brownies, 28, *29*
Nickelodeon Peanut Butter Bars, 30, *29*
Silk Stocking Almond Cookies, 26, *25*
Sugar House Frosted Cookies, 30
Tropical Gardens Cookies, 20
Tin Lizzie Oatmeal Treats, 22
"Uncle Sam-wiches", 24, *25*

Frostings, Fillings and Sauces
California Dream Chocolate Sauce, 79
Chocolate Glaze, 77
Classic Buttercream Cocoa Frosting, 78, *71*
Classic Chocolate Sauce, 79
Coconut Creme Filling, 62
Creamy Filling, 24
Creamy Mocha Frosting, 78
Eclair Filling, 47
Eclair Glaze, 47
Flower Power Fondue, 76
Let's Twist Again Fondue, 74, *75*
Lift-Off Fluffy Vanilla Frosting, 74

Lift-Off Fluffy Vanilla Frosting, 74
Memory-Making Fudge Frosting, 78
Mini Chip Filling, 66
Miniskirt Fondue, 76
"Mod" Nut-Chip Filling, 86
Moon Walk Peanut Butter Sauce, 79
New Frontier Carmel Frosting, 77
Pop Art Sugar Glaze, 87
Quick Chocolate Frosting, 79
Seven Minute Frosting, 76
Sixties Fondue Party, A, 74
Strawberry Whipped Cream Filling and Frosting, 60
Streusel, 93
Topping, 64
Very-Best-Ever Hot Fudge Sauce!, 77
Whipped Cream Filling, 78

Pies
Big Band Black Bottom Pie, 52, *53*
Chattanooga Choo-Choo Pie, 52, *53*
Classic Chocolate Cream Pie, 50
Crooner Cordial Pie, 55
Crumb Crust, 65
D-Day Hershey Bar Pie, 54
Elegant Chocolate Mousse Pie, 50, *51*
Graham-Nut Crust, 95
Home Front Coconut Cream Pie, 54, *53*
Macaroon-Nut Crust, 56
Our Gal Sundae Pie, 56, *57*

Puddings, Ice Creams and Other Treats
Back Porch Chocolate Ice Cream, 42
Better-Times Chocolate Pudding, 44, *45*
Big Apple Rum Souffle, 44, *45*
Blue Eagle Chocolate Bar Mousse, 43
Dreamy Choco-Nut Ice Cream, 40
Easy Chocolate Ice Cream, 43
Fireside Steamed Pudding, 46, *45*
Matinee Mint Parfaits, 42
Movie Palace Eclairs, 47, *45*
Swingtime Chocolate Mousse, 43
Top Hat Custard Ice Cream, 40, *41*

Microwave Sweets
Breakfast Bonus Muffins, 94
Double-Fun Pie, 95
Easy Mocha Freeze, 92
Kiss-Me-Quick Teacakes, 90
Microwave Cookie Favorites, 94
New-Fashioned Chocolate Mousse, 90, *91*
Space Age Mallow Glaze, 93
Time-Saver Streusel Cake, 93

Special Hershey Hints

A Hershey Frosting Hint, 31
Baking Terms, 94
Cookie Classifications, 26
Cookie Cues, 23
Do You Bake with Oven-proof Glassware?, 87
Easy Fruit Toppings, 70
General Baking Hints, 20
How to Frost a Layer Cake, 69
How to Measure Ingredients, 28
How to Melt Chocolate, 24
Important Microwave Hints, 92
Important Notes and Tips for Candy Makers, 8
Some Special Chocolate Decorations, 46
Storage Hints for Chocolate Products, 36, 95
Substitution Hints, 55-56
Thermometer Tips, 15
When is a Cake Done?, 60

Nostalgia Photographs: The Bettman Archive Inc.—pages 49 (right) and 59; Chicago Historical Society, lithograph, The Ferris Wheel—Midway Plaisance, W.C.E., 1893, artist: C. Graham—page 4; Culver Pictures Inc.—pages 2 (lower), 19, 33 (upper), 38, 39 (upper) and 73; Courtesy of Milton Hershey School Archives—pages 2 (upper), 5, 33 (lower), 39 (lower) and 48; H. Armstrong Roberts, Inc.—pages 18, 32, 49 (left), 58, 72, 81 (upper) and 88; Courtesy of Sears—page 3; United Press International Newspictures—pages 80, 81 (lower) and 89. *Photographs of Prepared Hershey Recipes:* Banner and Burns Inc.